Jagdverband 44
Squadron of *Experten*

OSPREY
PUBLISHING

Jagdverband 44
Squadron of *Experten*

Robert Forsyth

Series editor Tony Holmes

Front Cover

On 20 April 1945, Me 262s of *Jagdverband* 44 took off from their base at Munich-Riem to intercept B-26 Marauders of the USAAF's Ninth Air Force en route to bomb the marshalling yards at Memmingen, in southern Germany. The 48 aircraft of the 323rd Bomb Group (BG), led by Capt Lewis S Caldwell, were formed into three 'boxes' comprising eight six-aircraft flights, and were following a course from their base at Denain-Prouvy, in France, over the Rhine and into Bavaria. On the ground, JV 44's control room at Feldkirchen had picked up the bombers' approach and duly despatched a force of around 15 Me 262s, formed into individual *Ketten*, at 1030 hrs to intercept.

Shortly after 1100 hrs, JV 44's Me 262s were flying west in line astern in loose *Ketten* formation at between 3350-4000 metres when they observed the American bombers in clear skies over Kempten-Memmingen. The first *Kette* closed in on the Marauders from behind and the tail gunners began to open up as they attempted to keep the jets at bay. The Messerschmitt fighters' speed, combined with their lethal 30 mm guns, proved devastating, however.

This specially commissioned cover artwork by Mark Postlethwaite depicts JV 44's Me 262s at the moment of their fast pass through the formation. Three bombers were shot down and a further seven damaged in the attack (*Cover artwork by Mark Postlethwaite*)

FOR A CATALOGUE OF ALL BOOKS PUBLISHED BY OSPREY PLEASE CONTACT:

NORTH AMERICA
Osprey Direct, C/o Random House Distribution Centre, 400 Hahn Road, Westminster, MD 21157
Email: info@ospreydirect.com

ALL OTHER REGIONS
Osprey Direct, The Book Service Ltd, Distribution Centre, Colchester Road, Frating Green, Colchester, Essex, CO7 7DW
E-mail: customerservice@ospreypublishing.com

www.ospreypublishing.com

DEDICATION

I would like to dedicate this book to the memory of my mother, Muriel 'Lulu' Forsyth, who was an unshakeable example and true inspiration to me in every respect during the first 33 years of my life. I come to learn that more as every subsequent year passes

First published in Great Britain in 2008 by Osprey Publishing
Midland House, West Way, Botley, Oxford, OX2 0PH
443 Park Avenue South, New York, NY, 10016, USA
E-mail; info@ospreypublishing.com

CIP Data for this publication is available from the British Library

ISBN : 978 1 84603 294 3

Edited by Tony Holmes
Page design by Mark Holt
Cover Artwork by Mark Postlethwaite
Aircraft Profiles by Jim Laurier
Index by Alan Thatcher
Originated by PDQ Digital Media Solutions
Printed and bound in China through Bookbuilders
Typeset in Adobe Garamond and Univers

08 09 10 11 12 11   10 9 8 7 6 5 4 3 2

ACKNOWLEDGEMENTS

For their kind contribution during this 'second pass' at *Jagdverband* 44, the author would like to extend sincere thanks to Josef Dobnig, a former member of the unit, who so readily made available his recollections of his time with JV 44, and to Dr Wolfgang Dobnig for his helpful assistance during the writing of this book. I would also like to thank Eddie Creek, Nick Beale, Götz *Freiherr* von Richthofen, Richard Chapman, Tomás Poruba and Eric Mombeek for their kind help, guidance and suggestions.

EDITOR'S NOTE

To make this best-selling series as authoritative as possible, the Editor would be interested in hearing from any individual who may have relevant photographs, documentation or first-hand experiences relating to the world's elite pilots, and their aircraft, of the various theatres of war. Any material used will be credited to its original source. Please write to Tony Holmes via e-mail at: tony.holmes@zen.co.uk

CONTENTS

CHAPTER ONE
HEROES OR OUTCASTS? 6

CHAPTER TWO
FORMING UP 20

CHAPTER THREE
BATS OUT OF HELL 47

CHAPTER FOUR
RED AND WHITE RIDDLE 98

CHAPTER FIVE
MOUNTAIN KINGS 106

APPENDICES 122
COLOUR PLATES COMMENTARY 125
BIBLIOGRAPHY 127

INDEX 128

HEROES OR OUTCASTS?

To have experienced World War 2 during February 1945 as a senior German fighter commander serving on the Western Front and in the *Reichsverteidigung* (the aerial defence of the Reich) would have left one with a sense of depressing, and probably forbidding, metamorphosis.

The tide of war was ebbing relentlessly against Germany.

For these veteran commanders, there were, firstly, the immediate challenges in virtually every aspect of their lives – the daunting prospect of maintaining the morale of those under their command at a level high enough to continue to fight whilst deployed against an enemy with infinitely superior forces. They also had to sustain an acceptable level of operational efficiency amidst supply difficulties, if not shortages, in manpower, fuel, spares, ammunition and even food.

Then there was personal exhaustion, especially amongst leaders who had fought with success and distinction in air battles on virtually every front for four or five years – from Poland to England, from the Soviet Union and the Far North to Africa. True, there had been the accolades in the form of decorations and promotions, the glory and the fame, but at what cost? Thousands of their comrades left dead and the mental and physical toll on their own bodies and minds.

The process of metamorphosis from certain victory to what seemed irreversible defeat raised questions. Despite promises and assurances, the much vaunted V-weapons had not reversed the tide for Germany. News from the battlefronts in the Ardennes was not good either, as the last effort to close the Bastogne corridor had failed, causing von Rundstedt's offensive to stall. The situation in the East was not encouraging, either, with the Red Army having advanced on the Oder and encircled Budapest.

On the home front, German civilians had come to accept their grim lot, living under an endless rain of Allied bombs while, outnumbered and outgunned, the Luftwaffe struggled to take on the bombers which struck city after city, factory after factory, month after month.

The officers leading these hard-pressed fighter units must have questioned, most of them privately, the policies of their superiors and high-level commanders. Even the most hardened of their number must have occasionally averted their gaze from the eyes of the young and outwardly eager, but inwardly frightened and ill-trained, replacements who now replenished the ranks of the *Jagdverbände*.

But still they fought on.

In the early hours of New Year's Day, 1945, in an attempt to strike a decisive blow against the Allied tactical air forces, the Luftwaffe had launched a surprise low-level attack against 21 enemy airfields in North West Europe. Codenamed Operation *Bodenplatte*, it had been conceived under great secrecy by Generalmajor Dietrich Peltz, a highly decorated former bomber pilot who had been appointed to direct II. *Jagdkorps*, the main fighter command operating on the Western Front. Peltz was assisted by an experienced staff comprising fighter veterans Oberst Walter Grabmann, Oberst Hans Trubenbach and Oberstleutnant Gotthardt Handrick.

The attack deployed 41 *Gruppen* drawn from ten *Jagdgeschwader* and one *Schlachtgeschwader*, as well as Me 262 and Ar 234 jet bombers from KG 51 and KG 76 – in all a force of more than 900 aircraft. It was a monumental effort for the Luftwaffe to mount such an operation at this stage of the war. To the planners' credit, it achieved significant surprise, and – for a brief period – probably served to lift the spirits of many a war-weary or doubting *Jagdflieger*. It is believed that 388 Allied aircraft were destroyed or damaged as a result of *Bodenplatte*. The effects on the German side, however, were at best questionable and at worst very grave.

A total of 271 Bf 109s and Fw 190s were lost in the raid, with a further 65 damaged. Just under half of these fell to enemy anti-aircraft fire over frontline areas, while just under a quarter were shot down by Allied fighters. Those aircraft shot down, were, to a great extent, flown at low level by young, poorly-trained and inexperienced pilots who provided easy prey to Allied fighter pilots already airborne on early morning sorties.

In many cases, however, the German formations failed even to find their allocated targets, as with Oberstleutnant Johann Kogler's JG 6 over Volkel, whilst elsewhere they became lost or collided, as happened to Major Gerhard Michalski's JG 4 over Le Culot. In the latter case, of the 75 aircraft sortied by the *Jagdgeschwader*, only around 12-15 per cent of

The aftermath of Operation *Bodenplatte* for the Allies – the remains of a B-25 smoulders as a fire crew fights to dampen the flames at Melsbroek airfield on the outskirts of Brussels on 1 January 1945. This airfield was the target for a combined force from JG 27 and IV./JG 54, which succeeded in destroying some 50 Allied aircraft

the strike force actually attacked their assigned target, but the unit suffered a 47 per cent loss rate during the operation. This is comparable to JG 53, which lost 30 Bf 109s out of 80 attacking, or 48 per cent. Some 143 pilots were killed or listed as missing, with a further 21 wounded and 70 captured.

These debilitating figures included no fewer than three experienced *Geschwaderkommodore*, five *Gruppenkommandeur* and 14 *Staffelkapitäne*. Oberstleutnant Johannes Kogler, the *Kommodore* of JG 6, confessed to American interrogators after being shot down on 1 January 1945, 'Whatever we did was too soon or too late. One almost felt ashamed to go out in Luftwaffe uniform at home'.

In the dark aftermath of *Bodenplatte*, there were changes within the higher echelons of the *Jagdwaffe*, largely brought about by agitation from a small, but influential group of bomber commanders who had the ear of *Reichsmarschall* Hermann Göring. They had their own ideas about how the Luftwaffe fighter force should be run in the light of its apparent long-term mishandling under its existing leadership.

Göring, usually lying low in the sanctuary of his vast hunting estate at Carinhall on the Schorfheide, north of Berlin, where he could escape the pressures and criticisms directed at the Luftwaffe's performance emanating from the Nazi Party and the Army, was all too ready to listen to these officers. As the *Jagdwaffe* was striking the Allied airfields, Göring welcomed Peltz and fellow bomber pilot Oberstleutnant Hajo Herrmann, to his estate.

Herrmann, a *Ritterkreuzträger*, was not shy of radical ideas – he was the creator of the '*Wilde Sau*' nightfighter units, and would later develop *Schulungslehrgang Elbe*, an hoc formation using volunteer pilots for a massed ramming attack on American heavy bombers. Göring presented both officers with signed photographs and then invited them for a walk in the snow-covered grounds, as Herrmann has recorded in his memoirs;

'While I trudged beside Göring wearing my leather Luftwaffe coat and my short boots, my feet ice-cold, the others walked 50 paces behind. He embarked upon a long speech. He expressed his criticism of the fighter leadership, mentioning Galland as being one of them, as indeed he had done on other occasions. He said he had misjudged the bomber men. I listened in silence. Göring continued, "Peltz will take over the defence of the Reich. You will replace General Galland".'

Since the autumn of 1944, Göring's prestige with Hitler had sunk to an all time low. It appeared that the *Jagdwaffe* was incapable of defending its home airspace or protecting Germany's factories and cities. Losses amongst the *Jagdgeschwader* operating in the *Reichsverteidigung* were rising to nearly 30 per cent on every mission flown, while the number of victories

The aftermath of Operation *Bodenplatte* for the Luftwaffe – Gefreiter Alfred Michel of 16./JG 53 stares forlornly at the wreck of his Bf 109G-14, which was shot down by US anti-aircraft fire on his return flight from a mission to attack the Allied airfield at Metz-Frescaty. Michel's Bf 109 was just one of 271 precious German fighters downed on 1 January 1945. The *Jagdwaffe* would never recover from the losses suffered on this day

gained amounted to less than 0.2 per cent of Allied strength. Enemy fighters now virtually ruled the skies over Germany. Göring had to act – and act he did.

For a long time the *Reichsmarschall* had been dissatisfied with the accomplishments of his *General der Jagdflieger*, Generalleutnant Adolf Galland, and he saw him as the core reason for the ailing performance of the Luftwaffe fighter force. The fact that Galland had, since the summer of 1944, been endeavouring to preserve, consolidate and actually grow the Germany-based *Jagdgeschwader* in order to deploy some 2000 aircraft en masse in a knock-out blow against a major USAAF daylight raid was ignored.

Galland planned to build his reserve by bringing in scattered *Gruppen* from Austria and Italy so that a large force could be sent aloft to take on both the

bombers and the feared American fighter escorts all the way from northern Germany down to the Swiss border.

Training programmes were established so that the home defence units would be able to respond quickly and specifically to any one of a number of varying enemy air incursions – a network of emergency airfields was set up and communications between command centres and units improved.

Galland was prepared to sacrifice 400 aircraft and the lives of up to 150 precious pilots in order to bring down 400-500 heavy bombers in one so-called '*Grosse Schlag*' or Great Blow. Such losses in aircraft would mean the loss of 4000-5000 American aircrew, a blow from which even the USAAF would struggle to recover. By November 1944, the largest number of fighters fielded by the Luftwaffe in the West since 1940, drawn from eleven *Geschwader* and supplemented by day fighters on the Western Front as well as some 100 nightfighters in Denmark and southern Germany, was ready to take on the bombers.

In many respects, however, Galland's plans were unrealistic. His operation would have demanded high levels of coordination and commitment from large numbers of pilots whose abilities, in terms of training and experience, fell way short of the mark – such was the state of the *Jagdwaffe* by this stage of the war. Furthermore, Galland had not taken into account the *Führer's* plan for the Ardennes offensive, news of which reached him for the first time in December. His fighters would now be needed on the Western Front to support the forthcoming ground offensive. The path to *Bodenplatte* was set. Galland wrote in his diary;

'An offensive in the West was senseless. I knew that the insufficient training and lack of experience of our unit commanders meant the *Jagdwaffe* was doomed to failure.'

Following the disastrous results of Operation *Bodenplatte*, *Reichsmarschall* Hermann Göring decided to implement changes within the command of the Luftwaffe fighter force. It was a hasty attempt to seek a solution to what he perceived as shortcomings and failures which he wrongly believed were attributable to an inherent weakness – and even cowardice – on the part of the *Jagdwaffe's* commanders and pilots. Göring (left) is seen here at Lechfeld on 2 November 1943 with Professor Willy Messerschmitt (right), designer of the Me 262, during a flight demonstration of the Me 262 V6

ADOLF GALLAND

Adolf Galland was born on 19 March 1912 in West-erholt, Westphalia. The son of an estate manager, he spent his childhood in a middle-class rural home in an environment of strict religious discipline. He enjoyed sports and music rather than academic study, and at an early age developed a fondness for building wooden model aeroplanes. Qualifying as a glider pilot in 1931, Galland joined the fledgling Luft-waffe in 1933 and took part in a rudimentary and semi-clandestine training course for future German military airmen in Italy.

In April 1937 he volun-teered for more clandestine service, this time with the *Legion Condor* in Spain, where he flew He 51s as *Staffelkapitän* of 3./J 88 – not so much as the fighter pilot he wanted to be, but rather as a ground-attack flier, in which role he became instrumental in the development of close-support tactics. The regular reports that he despatched to his superiors were well received.

On his return from Spain in August 1938, the raven-haired, cigar-smoking young officer spent time working for the RLM, where Galland was involved in the establishment of the early *Schlacht-gruppen*, before flying 87 ground-support missions in Poland in a Hs 123 as a *Staffelkapitän* with II.(*Sch*)/LG 2. In February 1940, he finally made it onto Bf 109Es when sent to *Stab* JG 27 at Krefeld. Three months later, German forces attacked in the West. Although Galland found himself in a semi-administrative role drawing up pilot rosters, arranging unit-level meetings and liaising with *Fliegerkorps* VIII, JG 27's immediate command

organisation, he was still able to account for 12 aircraft destroyed by 9 June, including two Spitfires.

By then Galland had been transferred yet again, becoming *Gruppenkommandeur* of III./JG 26 at Capelle, in France. He led this unit with distinction during the battles against the RAF over the English Channel that summer.

In late August, Göring had decided to replace a number of those he deemed to be his older and more 'staid' unit commanders with younger, more innovative officers. It is perhaps not surprising that the exploits and accomplishments of the dashing, extrovert Adolf Galland, with his passion for hunting and shooting, should have attracted Göring, since he embodied all that was required of the modern fighter pilot.

On 22 August 1940, three weeks after he had been awarded the Knight's Cross with 17 victories to his credit, the newly promoted Major Galland was propelled to the position of *Kommodore* of JG 26, replacing Major Gotthardt Handrick, an officer whom Göring apparently disliked. Nevertheless, for his part, Galland had never been afraid to express his fears and misgivings to those in high command.

During the Battle of Britain, he took great pains to spell out to Göring the folly of trying to take on the Spitfire in turning dogfights in which he knew the RAF fighter enjoyed superior performance. Instead, Galland pushed for hit-and-run, nuisance tactics which gave the advantage to the fast Bf 109. As an innovator, he experimented with schemes as diverse as fitting telescopic sights into his cockpit to later masterminding the complex air-cover operation

Photo Caption
From 1937 through to late 1943, Adolf Galland enjoyed a meteoric rise through the ranks of the Luftwaffe from a *Staffelkapitän* with the *Legion Condor* in the Spanish Civil War to his appointment as *General der Jagdflieger* in November 1941. He is seen here in an official portrait from early 1942 with the rank of Oberst and wearing the Knight's Cross with Oakleaves and Swords and newly-awarded Diamonds – he was only the second recipient of this decoration

involving the successful escape of three of the *Kriegsmarine's* heavy ships from their enforced confinement in Brest to the sanctuary of the German coast, via the Straits of Dover, in broad daylight.

In November 1941, Galland, by now one of the few holders of the coveted Knight's Cross with Oakleaves and Swords (and the first recipient of the Swords), was plucked from his command of JG 26 to replace his 'old rival' Werner Mölders as *General der Jagdflieger* in the wake of the latter's death in an air crash while on his way to attend the funeral of Ernst Udet.

Under the quiet and capable direction of Mölders, an *Experte* in his own right with 115 confirmed aerial victories and holder of the coveted Diamonds to the Knight's Cross, the *Jagdwaffe* had embarked upon a programme of tactical development, primarily prompted by lessons learnt during the Spanish Civil War. Mölders had advocated a change in the standard tactical fighter formation used by the Luftwaffe, replacing the traditional three aircraft *Kette* with a more fluid and manoeuvrable two aircraft *Rotte* element.

Initially reluctant to relinquish his command of JG 26 for the 'politics' of senior command in Berlin, Galland nevertheless approached the inherent demands of his new appointment with due application. His efforts, however, frequently led to violent personality clashes with Göring, who began to view Galland's proposals for continuing Mölders' strengthening and reformation of the *Jagdwaffe* as indirect criticism of his own shortcomings. So it was that cracks and strains in the relationship between Göring and his fighter general began to appear as early as the spring of 1943.

When Galland endeavoured to point out the loss of manoeuvrability suffered by the outnumbered Bf 109s and Fw 190s based in the West as a result of

their carrying twin drop-tanks in order to increase flight duration, the *Reichsmarschall*, looking to save face with the *Führer*, ordered Galland to issue orders which forbade a pilot from jettisoning his tanks unless actually hit by enemy fire.

As Allied daylight raids intensified in late 1943, Galland chose to limit the number of missions flown by his *Reichsverteidigung* units against individual raids so as to allow sufficient repair and re-grouping of aircraft on emergency fields. Only by carefully conserving strength and by efficient management of its pilots could the *Jagdwaffe* hope to cause any damage to the US bombers. Göring paid scant heed to this theory and demanded that all available units be thrown against every raid.

As the *Jagdwaffe* began to suffer from attrition during late 1943, Göring believed that the lack of success against the Americans was attributable to a lack of courage on the part of his fighter pilots.

As Galland wrote in his post-war memoirs;

'Göring began to lay increasing blame on the *Jagdwaffe*, and as I felt I had earned the right to answer him back, we were soon at loggerheads. He proceeded to comment on the *Jagdwaffe's* lack of spirit. He may have been exasperated by my replies to his previous questions – at all events, he got into such a state that he hurled reproaches and accusations at us to the effect that we had been loaded with honours and decorations but had proved ourselves unworthy of them, that the *Jagdwaffe* had been a failure as early as the Battle of Britain and that many pilots with the highest decorations had faked their reports to get Knight's Crosses over England.'

In a moment of fury, Galland removed his own award and threw it down on the table. 'For six months after that I did not wear my decorations'.

Photo Caption
Galland looks on as an officer of the weapons and tactical evaluation unit *Eprobungskommando* 25 shows him equipment during a visit to Achmer on 17 November 1943. The unit was responsible for developing tactics and weapons for employment against USAAF heavy bombers. Immediately behind Galland is Hauptmann Horst Geyer, commander of E.Kdo 25, while visible at the rear is Major Hans-Günter von Kornatzki, commander of *Sturmstaffel* 1. By this time, Galland's prime concern was to arrest the level of attrition within fighter units defending Germany

Generalmajor Dietrich Peltz, the highly regarded and experienced former bomber and Stuka commander, whom, in late 1944, Göring favoured for assuming control of the defence of the Reich. He advocated the training of largely redundant bomber pilots for all-weather, jet fighter-bomber missions

He knew better than to argue. In any case, his position as commander of the *Jagdwaffe* was being gradually eroded by the bomber commanders, led by Peltz, Herrmann and Oberstleutnant Ulrich Diesing from the Luftwaffe Technical Office, who offered Göring fresh, innovative ideas. Peltz told Göring that redundant bomber pilots could be retrained to fly all-weather, jet fighter-bomber missions – and probably make a better job of it than the apparently overworked and exhausted fighter pilots.

Over Christmas week of 1944, Galland embarked on a tour of western-based *Jagdgruppen*. What he found shocked him;

'Units in the 3. *Jagddivision* area under (Generalmajor Walter) Grabmann were embittered about the leadership. The overall impression was shocking. I prepared a comprehensive report about my impressions, and the mistakes made, and submitted my proposals. This was my last travel report, and it sharply attacked the leadership of II. *Jagdkorps* for a number of evident leadership failures caused by a lack of experience in the command of fighter units.

'Everywhere I went I found shortcomings basically due to insufficient training and lack of experience on the part of the unit commanders. Added to this was the considerable indignation about the leadership's desultory manner of allocating responsibilities and expecting unit commanders to lead from their desks. My report was special, as it explained the reasons for the failure of the – numerically at least – extremely strong fighter units, and why the *Jagdwaffe* received a deadly blow during the Ardennes offensive ending in Operation *Bodenplatte*.'

It was probably this report that sealed Galland's fate. On his own initiative, before the end of the month he had already approached the Luftwaffe Chief-of-Staff, *General der Flieger* Karl Koller, 'to support my request for my return to operational service at the front'.

Shortly after making this request, however, during the course of a 'one-sided' two-and-a-half-hour telephone call from Göring, Galland was given the reasons why the *Reichsmarschall* had decided to sack him. 'Göring tried to blame me without really having a clear opinion himself', Galland recorded in his diary. 'Amongst other things, he reproached me for having a negative influence on fighter tactics, a lack of support and failure to enforce orders, for having created my own empire in the fighter arm, wrong staff policy, the removal of people I did not like and my responsibility for the bad state of the *Jagdwaffe*.

'I was not permitted to say a word in my defence. At the end, Göring expressed his gratitude, saying that after my leave, he would appoint me to an important position within the leadership. I said that this was not acceptable since under no circumstances would I want to be in a leading position now that the *Jagdwaffe's* collapse was imminent. I again requested to be employed operationally on the Me 262, not as a unit leader, but simply as a pilot. A decision was to be made during my leave.'

Galland subsequently left for his enforced period of leave 'embittered, depressed and without any definite plan for the future'.

By February 1945, as – backed by Göring – the influence of the 'new radicals' began to grip, a slow but perceptible transition took place within the command of the *Jagdwaffe*. The 'victims' of this transition included some of the Luftwaffe's most experienced and revered fighter leaders, whose services were, for one reason or another, no longer 'required'.

One of these victims was Oberstleutnant Johannes Steinhoff. Thirty-two-year-old 'Macki' Steinhoff was an accomplished veteran fighter pilot. A graduate in philology from the University of Jena in 1934, he subsequently attended both naval and Luftwaffe training schools.

Transferring to the Luftwaffe from the *Kriegsmarine* in 1936, Steinhoff embodied the ideal blend of social values and military discipline, and by 1938 had been given his first command as *Staffelkapitän* of 10(N)./JG 26. This was a hastily organised nightfighter unit equipped with the Bf 109C which, in December 1939 – having converted back to the day fighter role – engaged in the well-publicised attack on RAF Wellington bombers despatched to bomb warships at Wilhelmshaven. Steinhoff shot down a bomber in what became one of the earliest organised interceptions of a daylight bombing raid.

Steinhoff led 4./JG 52 during the fighting over the English Channel in 1940. His style of command was known to be fair-minded and professional, and he wasted little time in evicting from his *Staffel* a young Fähnrich by the name of Hans-Joachim Marseille whose somewhat overly casual demeanour he was unable to tolerate! Steinhoff was awarded the Knight's Cross for his 35th victory scored in Russia on 30 August 1941 and was appointed *Kommandeur* of II./JG 52 on 28 February 1942. By 31 August 1942, Steinhoff had chalked up 100 aerial kills, and he received the Oak Leaves two days later. His 150th victory came on 2 February 1943, and on the 24th of the following month he was transferred from the Eastern Front to Tunisia, where he assumed command of JG 77.

Within two days of taking over command of the *Geschwader*, Steinhoff shot down his first opponent in North Africa – a Spitfire. He led JG 77 from Africa through the maelstrom of the air combat over Sicily and Italy, engaging for the first time American heavy bombers and their escorts, against which his personal score continued to accumulate. In late July 1944, Steinhoff was awarded the Swords to his Knight's Cross to recognise his 167th aerial victory.

In November 1944, he was suddenly relieved of his command and recalled to the Reich, where he attended a conference organised by Göring at the *Luftkriegsakademie* Gatow. The aim of this meeting was to work out how best to 'restore the Luftwaffe to full striking power in the shortest possible time'.

In what became known as the '*Aeropag*', a carefully selected gathering of some 40 senior officers from the fighter, bomber, reconnaissance and ground-attack arms met in an attempt to resolve divisions and differences of opinions. Also present were several *National Sozialistische Flieger Offiziere* (National Socialist Party Flying Officers) and officers

Oberst Johannes Steinhoff, photographed in the Mediterranean during 1943 while *Kommodore* of JG 77. It was to Steinhoff whom Galland turned when forming *Jagdverband* 44

from the Technical Office and the Flight Test Centres, as well as the *Reichsmarschall's* personal staff. However, rather than solving issues, the conference – held in an air of acrimony and mistrust – simply served to heighten and worsen tensions between the key attendees.

Particularly in conflict were Galland and Oberstleutnant Gordon Gollob, the first fighter pilot to reach 150 confirmed victories, a former *Kommodore* of JG 77 and the third recipient of the Diamonds to the Knight's Cross. Galland had brought Gollob back from the frontline to serve on his staff as a regional fighter commander and specialist in technical development, but the relationship between Gollob and the *General der Jagdflieger* was never easy. As Galland recalled;

'I appointed him to my staff and entrusted him with full responsibilities for the preparation and planning for operational employment of the Me 262 and Me 163. Gollob did not tackle the task to my satisfaction. He was interested only in the purely technical aspects, neglecting ground organisation, the training of air- and groundcrews, setting up a communications network and the formation of operational units. This caused considerable friction between Gollob, myself and my staff.

'In the end, I had to monitor his work in detail and check whether my orders were being executed. Gollob did not like this at all. I therefore transferred him to the *Kommando der Erprobungsstellen*. He swore to take revenge on me and my staff! To this end, he teamed up with the bomber men to have me removed from my post, believing that I was too influential.'

This rapid deterioration in the relationship between the *General der Jagdflieger* and one of the most experienced and innovative, if not forceful, officers on his staff was to prove instrumental in promoting the growing sense of decay and spiritlessness that seeped through certain senior echelons of the *Jagdwaffe* in late 1944.

Steinhoff, a great supporter of Galland, was appalled, but he had new responsibilities, having been appointed *Kommodore* of the recently formed JG 7 – the first fighter unit to be equipped exclusively with the Me 262 jet fighter. III./JG 7 had been established at Lechfeld in mid-November as the initial component, with its flying and ground personnel largely being drawn from the disbanded KG 1 and the remains of *Kommando Nowotny*. The latter outfit was the ill-fated Me 262 operational evaluation unit which had ceased activity following the death of its eponymous commander, the highly decorated Austrian ace Major Walter Nowotny on 7 November 1944. Steinhoff was forced to work with what he was given, and it was meagre.

By the end of the month III./JG 7 had just 11 Me 262s on strength against the promised figure of 40. Eventually, in January 1945, the *Gruppe* reached its intended strength of 40 pilots, with the 9., 10. and 11. *Staffeln* transferring to their operational bases at Parchim, Oranienburg and Brandenburg-Briest, respectively. However, although pilot availability was acceptable, aircraft availability was still painfully lacking, with only 19 Me 262s being recorded on strength on 19 January.

For Steinhoff, by this time the situation in JG 7 had become academic, since events had taken a dramatic twist. In December, after barely five weeks in the post, he was relieved of his command on the grounds of 'inactivity', and his place taken by Major Theo Weissenberger, a fellow *Ritterkreuzträger* and formerly the *Kommandeur* of I./JG 5.

Steinhoff recalled in one of his memoirs, 'It was in a mood of wretched depression that I collected together the last of my things the morning after my "dismissal". What bothered me was the idea that, with the war sliding hopelessly towards catastrophe, I could not fly any more, could not lead my Group any more. An officer without a command, I was virtually non-existent. It was as if I had been killed in action'.

Apart from 'inactivity', Steinhoff's crime had been to become an instrumental member of a small group of Germany's finest fighter commanders who were outraged at the humiliating way in which the 'Galland affair' had been handled.

The group was led by Oberstleutnant Günther Lützow, *Kommandeur* of IV. *Fliegerschuledivision*. Lützow came from a Prussian family with a long lineage of soldiers and men of the cloth. During his service with the *Legion Condor* in Spain, he had recorded the first ever aerial victory in the Bf 109, and in November 1939 Lützow had transferred from the *Jagdfliegerschule* at Werneuchen, where he had been involved with training future *Jagdflieger*, to take over I./JG 3, which he led until August 1940. On 21 August he was appointed *Kommodore* of JG 3, and duly led the '*Udet*' *Geschwader* through the Battle of Britain and on the Russian Front, where he became recognised, along with Mölders, as a first-class formation commander and tactician.

Oberst Günther Lützow (far left), recipient of the Knight's Cross with Oakleaves and Swords, was the second German fighter pilot to be credited with 100 victories. He later served as Inspector of the Fighter Arm under Adolf Galland. Lützow is seen here in conversation with Focke-Wulf designer Dr Kurt Tank (in short-sleeved shirt). Lützow would eventually fall foul of Göring for his critical and outspoken views on the leadership of the Luftwaffe

Lützow became only the second German fighter pilot to be credited with 100 victories, having by then already been decorated with the Swords to the Knight's Cross with Oakleaves on 11 October 1941 after claiming his 92nd victory. Following a period as Galland's *Inspekteur der Jagdflieger*, he was then given command of the 1. *Jagddivision* from November 1943 to March 1944, in which capacity he became responsible for day and nightfighter operations in northwest Germany and the Low Countries. Lützow was one of the most highly regarded officers in the *Jagdwaffe*, known for his calm, but straightforward, manner.

Other officers were persuaded to rebel against Göring, whom, they felt, was being influenced by aggressively ambitious personalities. Amongst those railing against the *Reichsmarschall* were Oberst Gustav Rödel (formerly *Kommodore* of JG 27 with 98 victories at war's end, and a recipient of the Knight's Cross and Oakleaves), Oberst Günther von Maltzahn (former commander of fighters in Italy with 68 victories at war's end, and a recipient of the

Oberst Lützow (standing), the architect of the so-called 'Fighter Pilot's Mutiny', expressed outrage at the way in which Galland (seated to Lutzow's right) was forced from his position as *General der Jagdflieger*, and he assembled a group of like-minded fighter commanders with whom he eventually organised an audience with Göring in order to protest. This photograph was taken at a conference in 1944

Knight's Cross and Oakleaves) and Oberst Hannes Trautloft (formerly *Kommodore* of JG 54 and the *Inspizient Ost* on Galland's staff with 57 victories at war's end, and a bearer of the Knight's Cross).

Throughout January 1945, by means of semi-covert meetings with a number of Luftwaffe generals and even senior SS officers, the Lützow 'mutineers' attempted to force a confrontation with Göring, at which time they intended to put forward their grievances and demand Galland's reinstatement. This proved unsuccessful, and on 23 January, Göring officially announced Galland's dismissal, and his successor;

'Generalleutnant Galland has been dismissed from his post following several years service as *General der Jagdflieger*, in order that he may once again be deployed in command once his health has been restored. I wish to express my sincere thanks to Generalleutnant Galland for his services performed on behalf of myself, for the German *Jagdwaffe* and for the Fatherland. With untiring zeal in both operations and administration, Galland has fulfilled the aims of the *Jagdwaffe*. In place of Generalleutnant Galland, I have appointed Oberst Gollob to safeguard the duties of the *General der Jagdflieger*. I expect that the *Jagdwaffe* will support Oberst Gollob. It should be remembered that it is neither the organisation nor the man that is important, but only the goal that is common to us all – the regaining of air supremacy over German territory.'

Retribution was meted out swiftly from the *Reichsmarschall's* offices. Lützow was despatched to 'exile' in Italy, where he assumed the position of *Jafü Oberitalien*, but from where he would no longer be able to extend influence. Other officers associated with Lützow were placed under watch.

Even away from the intrigue, there were a few senior officers with impressive combat records who had clashed with Göring and paid the price. At 31 years of age, Oberstleutnant Heinz Bär was *Kommodore* of JG 3 '*Udet*'. Bär was one of the *Jagdwaffe's* most experienced and accomplished combat pilots. His service career stretched back to 1939 –

Oberstleutnant Heinz Bär was one of the Luftwaffe's most accomplished *Jagdflieger* and unit commanders, and by war's end he had achieved around 220 aerial victories. In mid-1944, however, his bluntness failed to 'impress' Göring, who quietly transferred him away from frontline command and assigned him to lead the Me 262 training and conversion *Gruppe* III./EJG 2. He is seen here sitting on the outer wing of his Me 262 'Red 13' at Lechfeld while with that unit

the year he scored his first victory in the west. Concluding the Battle of Britain with 17 confirmed victories, Bär subsequently flew in Russia with JG 51, and within two months had accumulated 60 kills. The award of the *Ritterkreuz* came in July 1941, followed by the Oakleaves in August – a month which saw him down six Soviet aircraft in one day.

Leaving Russia in 1942, he was given command of I./JG 77, with whom he flew over Sicily, Malta and North Africa, claiming another 45 victories and gaining the Swords to the *Ritterkreuz*, despite contracting a punishing bout of malaria and being stricken by gastric ulcers. Some sources also state that Bär's fighting spirit took a dent following these illnesses, and matters were not helped by his apparently difficult relationship with Steinhoff, the *Geschwaderkommodore* of JG 77.

In the summer of 1943, after a number of confrontations with Steinhoff, he was transferred to France for apparent 'cowardice before the enemy', where he took over command of an operational training unit, *Jagdgruppe Süd*. One Luftwaffe airman commented of Bär;

'Actually, from what one has heard about Bär, he was a "tough" who was avoided as much as possible by the officer corps.'

Ill and exhausted by endless combat, Bär returned to Germany for a period of convalescence, before embarking on a long, hard stint as one of the foremost operational commanders in the Defence of the Reich. However, once home, his plain speaking on tactical policies did not enamour him to Göring, who saw fit to 'demote' him – thus his first posting in Germany was as a 'mere' *Staffelkapitän*. Tenacity, and an undeniable combat record, however, meant that it was not long before Bär was once again entrusted with more senior command and appointed *Kommandeur* of II./JG 1.

By mid-1944 he had been appointed to lead JG 3, flying regular missions against USAAF heavy bombers. On 1 January 1945, the day of *Bodenplatte*, Bär led his *Geschwader* successfully in an attack on Eindhoven airfield, in Holland, which was home to a number of Typhoon, Spitfire and Mustang squadrons of the 2nd Tactical Air Force (TAF). On 13 February, however, he was transferred away from operations to take command of Me 262 training unit III./EJG 2 in the relatively 'quiet' area of Lechfeld, in southern Germany.

Of Bär's final tally of around 220 aerial victories at the war's end, as many as 22 are believed to have been four-engined bomber kills.

Then there were those who simply found themselves unemployed.

Walter Krupinski had flown more than 1100 operational missions in which he had been accredited with 197 confirmed aerial victories, having been five times wounded, bailed out on four occasions and undergone numerous crash landings. By March 1945, Krupinski had effectively been made redundant by the continual regroupings and redesignations of the various Luftwaffe fighter *Geschwader*. With no prospect of a satisfactory posting, it was his destiny to sit out the remaining weeks of the war in a fighter pilots' rest home.

Born in Domnau, East Prussia, in November 1920, '*Graf*' Krupinski was an indomitable Prussian figure, and one of the *Jagdwaffe's* most successful aces on the Eastern Front, where, between September 1941 and March 1944, he was credited with 177 aerial victories. But it had been a long and hard road getting there. He had assumed his first operational posting with 6./JG 52 in the West in the autumn of 1940 and commenced what was to become a long and highly successful association with that *Geschwader*.

Initially, despite Krupinski's best efforts, success over the enemy eluded him. His first encounter proved a failure when he and his squadronmate, Leutnant Gerd Barkhorn, chased a lone Bristol Blenheim across the English Channel. Despite exhausting their ammunition, neither pilot was able to hit the elusive RAF reconnaissance aircraft and eventually they were forced to turn for home. It was an inauspicious start for two pilots who, between them, would eventually notch up nearly 500 victories.

Krupinski finally scored his first kill in late 1941 against a Russian long-range DB-3 bomber south of Leningrad. By the end of that year, his tally stood at just seven enemy aircraft, but following a short rest in Germany in early 1942, his fortunes were about to change. Returning to Russia, having worked hard to improve his gunnery skills, Krupinski quickly increased his personal score to 66 enemy aircraft destroyed, and in May 1942 he was awarded the *Ehrenpokal*.

After being wounded and hospitalised, Krupinski spent a brief time as a fighter instructor in France. Returning to Russia, his rapidly increasing score saw the award of the Knight's Cross on 29 October, by which time he had accounted for virtually every type of Russian frontline aircraft. On one day in July 1943 he scored 11 victories, going on to achieve his 150th kill by mid-October.

Oberleutnant Walter Krupinski posed for this informal photograph soon after receiving the Oakleaves to his Knight's Cross on 2 March 1944 in recognition of his 177 aerial victories, scored during the course of 1000 combat missions

Krupinski left JG 52 in March 1944 to return to the homeland to take up command of 1./JG 5, flying the Bf 109 in the *Reichsverteidigung*. After accounting for a B-17, two P-51s and a P-47, and having been awarded the Oakleaves to the Knight's Cross, he was transferred again, this time as *Gruppenkommandeur* of II./JG 11 at Hustedt. With the D-Day invasion of 6 June 1944, the *Gruppe* was one of those rushed to Normandy, where it operated from makeshift strips undertaking low-level missions against the advancing Allied armies. Krupinski went on to claim another ten Allied fighters destroyed during this period, including three P-51s, before his Bf 109 exploded in mid-air. Miraculously, Krupinski survived, but he was hospitalised once again.

Having recovered from his wounds, Krupinski was transferred to Oberstleutnant Josef Priller's JG 26 in early October 1944, taking command of the Bf 109-equipped III. *Gruppe* at Plantlünne. It was to be a challenging position made worse by a long, cold autumn of attrition, with the whole of JG 26 deployed along the German-Dutch border opposing Spitfires and Typhoons of the 2nd TAF. The weather over northwest Europe hampered operations, and the *Jagdwaffe* was still reeling from the effects of *Bodenplatte*. Although Krupinski's *Gruppe* was eventually re-equipped with the much-vaunted Fw 190D-9, on 25 March it was unexpectedly disbanded. He subsequently recalled;

'At that time it had become very clear that due to pilot and aircraft availability, as well as the fuel situation, the *Geschwader* could not support four *Gruppen* any longer, and Priller decided that one would have to be disbanded. It was decided that it would be III. *Gruppe*. Priller bade me farewell, but as a gesture of goodwill, ordered me to go to Lechfeld to ask (Heinz) Bär, who was commanding III./EJG 2, if and when my *Gruppe* could convert to the Me 262. That was my official instruction.

'I drove down to Lechfeld early next morning in one of those little wood-burning cars, and I arrived there about lunchtime. I went straight to Bär, whom I had known for a long time before, and asked whether it might be possible for my *Gruppe* to be incorporated into his unit and convert to the Me 262. Bär burst out laughing. There was no way he could accommodate us. He needed months to convert the pilots he already had, let alone us. So, I shrugged and left.'

At that point it seems Krupinski decided to 'call it quits' and made his way to Bad Wiessee, where he intended to remain as long as possible, preferably to the end of the war. He was mentally and physically exhausted after continuous action since 1940;

'I decided to go down to Bad Wiessee, where we had our fighter pilot recreation centre, and finish the war there where I could still enjoy a few drinks and some good food.'

It was thus the case that by March 1945, for whatever reasons, the Luftwaffe High Command considered it appropriate, one way or another, to effectively make redundant no fewer than four of Germany's finest fighter commanders – Steinhoff, Lützow, Bär and Krupinski – who, collectively by war's end, would have flown some 3300 combat missions and claimed 701 aerial victories. But a greater irony was to come, for within the space of just a few weeks, these men would be flying in operations once again, under Adolf Galland, in a unit like no other, equipped with the world's most revolutionary fighter aircraft.

FORMING UP

I n late January 1945, while a depressed Adolf Galland languished under effective house arrest in a Berlin apartment contemplating shooting himself, his successor as *General der Jagdflieger*, Oberst Gordon Gollob, set about arranging to post the sacked fighter general to the northern sector of the Eastern Front. It was intended that he would take command of the Fw 190s of 4./JG 54, which were flying support missions for German forces trapped in the Kurland pocket. This was considered to be suitably 'out of the way'.

Luckily for Galland, however, Gollob's intentions were frustrated by a call from a most unexpected quarter. Before Gollob could make the necessary arrangements, Galland was summoned to the Reichs Chancellery for an audience with Adolf Hitler.

Reporting as ordered, Galland was informed apologetically by Hitler's Luftwaffe adjutant, Oberst von Below, that the *Führer* had been detained elsewhere. It transpired that an investigation launched into Galland's affairs by the *Sicherheitsdienst* (the Security Service) had been stopped by the *Führer* himself. It seems that Galland was still held in favour in certain influential quarters, for Albert Speer, Hitler's armaments minister, is known to have protested to Hitler about the way in which Galland had been treated – his car had been seized, his movements monitored, his telephone wire tapped and his orderly questioned.

Under such circumstances, Galland could see salvation only in returning to an operational role, flying the aircraft which he considered to offer the best possible counter-force to the Allied heavy bomber threat – Messerschmitt's Me 262 jet-powered interceptor. It had been as long ago as May 1943 that he had flown the Me 262 V4 prototype at Lechfeld and

The Me 262 V3 prototype PC+UC is seen here at Leipheim in 1943 after having been rebuilt following an accident during trials the previous year. The aircraft reached unprecedented test speeds in the autumn of 1943, and Adolf Galland went to great efforts to convince his superiors in the Luftwaffe that the jet fighter offered both significant technical and tactical opportunities

immediately recognised in its revolutionary new design that this was the aircraft which Germany desperately needed to win the initiative in the air war over Europe. Indeed, he commented to observers on the ground after his flight that 'It felt as if angels were pushing'!

Thanks to the Me 262's high speed – the V3 reached 950 kmh during tests in October 1943 – and tactical potential, Galland became a firm advocate for its further development. He wrote enthusiastically to his superiors that all measures should be taken to ensure swift and large-scale production of the aircraft. In a report to the *Generalluftzeugmeister* Erhard Milch he wrote, 'The aircraft represents a great step forward, and could be our greatest chance – it could guarantee us an unimaginable lead over the enemy if he adheres to the piston engine'.

Despite teething problems with the Me 262's ailerons, rudders, stability and fuel injection, Galland pushed for the cancellation of the Me 209 project, which was intended as the replacement for the Bf 109, in favour of the jet-powered Messerschmitt fighter. Eventually, by the autumn of 1944, Galland's efforts had resulted in the formation of *Kommando Nowotny* – an Me 262 operational evaluation unit under the command of Austrian fighter ace Major Walter Nowotny which was intended to demonstrate the benefit of mass deployment of the Me 262 as a fighter, rather than as a fighter-bomber as Hitler desired.

There were problems from the start. Following a somewhat crude training programme, it was found that only 15 pilots – those possessing any experience at all on the type – were capable of flying the jet. Nevertheless, by late September *Kommando Nowotny* had 30 Me 262s.

The following month saw the commencement of limited combat operations, but in the first half of October, no fewer than ten jets were either destroyed or damaged due to take-off or landing accidents. Nowotny's pilots, most of them drawn from conventional single-engined fighter units, lacking sufficient training in instrument flying and with only two or three intended training flights, found the Me 262 with its effortless speed, short endurance and rapid descent, difficult to handle.

Worse was to come when Galland, already concerned at the increasing losses being suffered by his only jet fighter unit, arrived at Achmer on 7 November for an inspection. The next day, as the USAAF bombed the

Me 262s of *Kommando Nowotny* – the Luftwaffe's first truly operational jet fighter unit – at Achmer in the autumn of 1944. Named after its Austrian commander, Major Walter Nowotny, an acclaimed holder of the Oakleaves to the Knight's Cross and former *Kommandeur* of II./JG 26, the unit's pilots struggled to master the jet's speed and general handling characteristics. Many of its aircraft were damaged or destroyed in accidents or shot down in early combat operations as a result

Nordhorn Canal and the marshalling yards at Rheine, the *Kommando* was able to despatch just four jets in two missions against the bombers.

In the second mission Nowotny himself took off to engage the enemy, but a short while later his voice was heard over the radio. 'We stepped into the open', Galland later wrote. 'Visibility was not good – six-tenths cloud. Seconds later an Me 262 appeared out of the cloud and dived vertically into the ground. There was black smoke and an explosion'. Nowotny's last words, though garbled, indicated that his aircraft was on fire, and seconds later, in front of a horrified Galland, he crashed to his death.

Despite attempts by Dietrich Peltz to secure the Me 262 as a high-speed bomber, Galland fought a determined battle to deploy the jet in its most obvious role – as a fighter interceptor graced with the speed to evade numerically superior Allied fighters. The jet was also equipped with four nose-mounted 30 mm MK 108 cannon capable of shooting down heavy bombers with relatively little ammunition expenditure. In this view, Galland was supported by many senior fighter commanders, including Major Gerhard Stamp, the commander of I./JG 300, which provided high-altitude fighter cover for the heavily-armoured Fw 190-equipped *Sturmgruppen* in the defence of the Reich. In a report prepared for senior commanders in November 1944, Stamp wrote;

'The solution to the problem of successful defence lies in counteraction against enemy fighters, which are superior in both numbers and performance. These considerations lead to the conclusion that a change in the air situation over the Reich is not possible with the forces presently available. If, on the other hand, the Luftwaffe could operate in sufficient strength with these new types of aircraft, then we might effectively beat the enemy's fighters and thus bring about a change in the whole situation. The single-seat Me 262 is capable of fulfilling these expectations.'

Despite the fact that by January 1945 the first Me 262-equipped *Jagdgruppe* (III./JG 7 under the command of Major Erich Hohagen) was still forming up at bases around Berlin, Galland must have felt a sense of weary satisfaction when von Below informed him of Hitler's decision instructing him to establish a unit equipped with the Me 262. At last he would able to prove once and for all that it was the 'superior' aircraft he said it was. To this end, Galland was told to report to Göring at Carinhall to be issued with further orders.

A few days later, Galland drove to the *Reichsmarschall's* estate, around which could be heard the sound of artillery thundering away to the east as the Red Army pressed home its winter offensive across the Oder. Galland found the *Reichsmarschall* to be truculent and forthright, but untruthful. Göring – ignorant of Galland's discussions with von Below – claimed to have had all the accusations aimed at his former *General der Jagdflieger* silenced, but still carped on that Galland had failed him. As Galland later recorded, Göring would allow him one last chance;

'I was to set up a small unit to demonstrate that the Me 262 was the superior fighter that I had always claimed it was. A small unit only in *Staffel* strength was to be organised – any more than that would not be possible. I would have to find the aircraft myself. He told me that Oberst Steinhoff, whom he had dismissed, and whom he had considered to be a "sad case", could be made available to me, and that Oberst Lützow would be available immediately, if I wanted him. I was to submit my proposals.

'The unit was not to be under the command of any division, corps or air fleet – I was to be totally independent. However, there was to be no contact between the new unit and any other fighter or jet unit.'

Yet it was to his American interrogators in June 1945 that Göring later admitted that the relatively weak air defence of southern Germany had given him cause for concern. 'Mustangs were practically doing training flights over Bavaria', he had confessed. Thus, he had recalled Galland in order to stop that 'nonsense'.

Galland thanked Göring, bade him farewell and returned to Berlin. On the way back to the capital, he mused over the fact that Göring had also given him free rein to call his new unit whatever he wished – providing it did not hold any connotations with the name 'Galland'! He therefore decided upon '*Jagdverband* 44', which would abbreviate to 'JV 44' – an indirect and ironic reminder of the year of his dismissal, as well as a number which amounted, coincidentally, to exactly half of the number of the designation of the very first fighter unit in which had ever served, J 88, in Spain.

Left entirely alone, a few days later he set up a small office at Kladow, between Gatow and Potsdam on the western bank of the Havel. From there he began the task of setting up his unit. For a man who had organised and commanded an entire fighter force, the prospect of forming a *Staffel* would have seemed relatively undemanding. His first move was to find an airfield that would be suitable for jet operations.

After inspecting a number of facilities, he eventually settled on Brandenburg-Briest, some 50 kilometres west of Berlin. The fact that Briest already served as the base for III./JG 7 operating in the defence of Berlin was testimony in itself, apart from the fact that it was protected by ample flak batteries and was within reasonable distance of an Me 262 aircraft park.

Meanwhile, Göring's promise of autonomy was not quite as it seemed, for on 10 February 1945, Gollob issued instructions that the Fw 190-equipped IV./JG 54 was to be disbanded and reformed as the new second *Gruppe* of JG 7 under Major Hermann Staiger at Landsberg. One *Staffel* of the *Gruppe* was to be assigned to Galland – not to test the Me 262 in combat, but rather as a jet training unit for NCO pilots. Happily for Galland though, once again Gollob's orders were not effected.

A short while later, between 23-25 February, Galland discussed his personnel, aircraft and equipment requirements with officers from the staff of the Luftwaffe Chief of General Staff, *General der Flieger* Karl Koller.

As the *Verbandskommandeur*, and with some degree of ambition, Galland proposed the creation of a sophisticated 'self-supportive' unit with a nominal strength of 16 Me 262s, 15 pilots, a Jumo engine technician, a specialist from Messerschmitt, mechanics, engine fitters and armourers. Such numbers would allow Galland to create two small four-jet *Staffeln* and a *Gruppenstab* equipped with a further eight aircraft. These would be supported by motor transport (to include heavy, medium and light personnel carriers, light vehicles, trailers and bicycles), signals (with radio and cable specialists), aircraft and weapons servicing (to include drivers, light vehicles, battery and generator trucks and trailers), meteorological, administration and medical sections.

Adolf Galland prepares to aim his hunting rifle to shoot at ducks on the Havel, not far from JV 44's base at Brandenburg-Briest, in March 1945. Behind Galland, in the centre of the photograph, is Oberst Johannes Steinhoff, the recently departed *Kommodore* of JG 7

Galland got most of what he wanted because, soon after, Koller authorised the establishment of JV 44 'with immediate effect' on the basis that a cadre of pilots would be provided through the normal channels, while ground personnel would be provided from 16./JG 54 (which was in the process of being redesignated as 7./JG 7). Koller further ordered that aircraft were to be supplied to the unit 'with all speed'. However, the structure of JV 44 was to be cut back by the loss of a Meteorologist and a Weapons Technician from the *Stab* and by some reductions in motor transport, although a minimal fleet of field cars, motorcycles, bicycles and trailers would be allowed to remain.

Galland was ready to go to war – almost. Now he needed his key personnel. His immediate requirement was for a highly experienced officer capable of building up the unit and coordinating personnel from training through to operations. Without hesitation, he contacted his friend Johannes Steinhoff, who had recently been replaced as *Kommodore* of JG 7 by Major Theo Weissenberger.

Steinhoff had just returned to Germany from an attempt to visit Lützow in Italy, and upon his arrival in Berlin he was instructed by Hauptmann Hugo Kessler (one of Galland's aides) to make his way to Brandenburg-Briest, where he was to meet with Galland. After some brief discussions, Steinhoff was 'recruited' – willingly! He subsequently recorded in his memoirs;

'It was my third posting in Brandenburg in five years of war. This time, it was not as the commander of a fighter group, but rather as a kind of "maid-of-all-work". We threw ourselves into the task with the same spirit and enthusiasm that had characterised the early days of the Luftwaffe, but the early days of *Jagdverband* 44 were far from being days of plenty. Our transport, for example, consisted of a single jeep and my tiny 90cc DKW motorcycle, which I had contrived to get assigned to us.

'My old unit, JG 7, was stationed on the same airfield, but they had orders from Galland's successor not to lift a finger to help us. For the most part they just ignored us, though there was the occasional smile of condescending sympathy for the "mutineers". One or two of my former comrades looked as if they had a sneaking admiration for us, but they were probably under pressure not to show it. The vast majority of those who saw us pottering about the airfield, training busily, thought we were quite simply mad. The general, however, had influential friends, and we soon found ourselves on the receiving end of a swelling supply of equipment, aircraft, spares and weapons. We even got a second jeep. JG 7 asked for my motorcycle back, so I buzzed across the airfield on it and told them they couldn't have it.'

With Steinhoff installed, Galland next began a process of 'business and pleasure'. Alongside the occasional duck-hunting excursion on the Havel and the Schwielowsee, he drew up a wish-list of pilots whom he considered to be adept enough to convert quickly to the Me 262. The list included some of the *Jagdwaffe's* most skilled and successful formation leaders and pilots such as Lützow, Trautloft, Hartmann and Späte.

Major Wolfgang Späte was the *Kommodore* of JG 400, which operated the Me 163 rocket-powered interceptor over central and northern Germany in defence of the oil refineries. A recipient of the Oakleaves to the Knight's Cross, Späte had been one of Germany's most famous sailplane pilots, and had later accumulated 90 victories over the Eastern Front with JG 54. By the early spring of 1945, however, JG 400 was struggling to continue operations with its Me 163s owing to restrictions in fuel, ground-handling equipment and transport.

Plans were drawn up to transfer the *Geschwader's* personnel to JG 7, and it was with some surprise that Späte received a telephone call from Oberstleutnant Gollob, who offered him the choice of flying the Me 262 with JG 7 or joining Galland's fledgling unit. He chose JG 7, largely because he had known Weissenberger, its commander, from his gliding days before the war. 'On the other hand', Späte later recalled, 'I held a deep respect for Galland, and the opportunity of flying with a unit under his guidance was tempting. I admired him, not least, because having been unjustly fired by Göring, he didn't simply hide away, hurt and moaning. Rather, he built up a flying unit the size of a *Staffel*, went into action and defended his country to the very last day. It was exemplary!'

But Gollob proved to be not so open-hearted when it came to other pilots. Galland complained post-war that the *General der Jagdflieger* 'did everything to cross and counteract my wishes and proposals. Because of this and other reasons – mostly because of a lack of communication – not all the pilots I wanted in JV 44 showed up at Brandenburg-Briest'.

Generalleutnant Adolf Galland, the newly appointed commander of *Jagdverband* 44, takes a break from his duties at Brandenburg-Briest to enjoy some sailing on the Havel in March 1945. To the right, partially obscured by the sailing boat's wheelhouse and holding the tiller and rope, is Oberst Johannes Steinhoff, Galland's second-in-command

Oberstleutnant Gordon Gollob was appointed *General der Jagdflieger* – as such, Galland's successor – in January 1945. Gollob, who had served on Galland's staff, was a highly experienced fighter pilot, a former *Geschwaderkommodore* and holder of the coveted Diamonds to the Knight's Cross with Oakleaves and Swords. Yet he was apparently very critical in nature, and he and Galland suffered extreme friction in their relationship

The view from the office of the *General der Jagdflieger* offered a different perspective as Gollob recalled;

'At exactly the moment when Galland and everyone else in the Luftwaffe knew that there was a shortage of experienced formation leaders, this gentleman in no way held back from requesting for himself – without exception – our aces. But he only got those I let him have, and a few that he "organised" for himself by roundabout methods.

'The list of pilots which Galland compiled for "his" JV 44 when he was no longer *General der Jagdflieger* was simply a wish list. What do you think would have happened had I pulled all of these experienced formation leaders out of their units to put them at Galland's disposal? It was for that reason that, in many cases, I refused, and so he got only a part of the nominated pilots and formation leaders, among them those who, unfortunately, were in disgrace or those who, for other reasons, could not or did not wish to remain with their units.'

Furthermore, Gollob expressly prevented JV 44 from 'influencing' any other units. Yet at the same time Galland was aware that Göring was expecting to see results. Fortunately, a number of Galland's erstwhile senior staff officers such as Oberst Hannes Trautloft held positions of influence.

Trautloft, who had recently assumed command of the 4. *Fliegerschule-division* from Günther Lützow, engineered the transfer of a number of experienced flying instructors to JV 44 – men who, despite extended periods away from operational flying, nevertheless relished the chance for an opportunity to fly the Me 262 before the war drew to an end. Ignoring Gollob, Galland also worked hard to attract as many unit commanders as he could, although this proved challenging, and the reality was that in many cases he would have to settle for exhausted men recovering from long periods of combat, or those recovering from wounds.

The exact circumstances in which Galland obtained the services of Major Karl-Heinz Schnell remain unknown, but it is likely that he was one of the first of what became a steady trickle of experienced frontline formation commanders to join JV 44 over the next few weeks.

'Bubi' Schnell, from Essen, had flown with JG 51 since the outbreak of war, initially with II. *Gruppe* before transferring to III./JG 51, with whom he fought during the French campaign of 1940. Appointed *Staffelkapitän* of 9./JG 51 on 1 October 1940 shortly after the battle against the RAF over the English Channel, Schnell then served in Russia, and was awarded the Knight's Cross on the occasion of his 29th victory on 1 August 1941, soon after the German invasion.

Following a period at a fighter school in France, he was appointed to lead III./JG 51 in mid-1942 when its then *Kommandeur*, Hauptmann Richard Leppla, was wounded. Schnell would stay in command until June 1943 when, as a result of lingering problems caused by wounds suffered in combat, he took up a staff position with the RLM overseeing the activities of the fighter schools. He was later assigned to command JG 102, but his wounds continued to trouble him, and when Johannes Steinhoff's offer of a place with the new unit came about, Schnell was actually in hospital. However, the veteran of 500 missions needed little urging to leave.

It was officers such as Schnell, who by the end of the war would be accredited with 72 victories, 11 of which were scored in the West, that Galland hoped would form the backbone of JV 44.

Already stationed at Brandenburg-Briest, but quickly following Schnell to Galland's ranks, was 29-year-old Major Erich Hohagen. Also in and out of hospital, Hohagen had relinquished his command of III./JG 7 at Brandenburg to Major Rudolf Sinner just a month prior to joining JV 44, the ace having chosen to step down during a period of relative operational inactivity in the *Gruppe's* establishment.

Hohagen was regarded as one of the *Jagdwaffe's* true frontline veterans, having accumulated several thousand hours flying some 60 different types, and having seen continuous action on the Channel Front in 1940, during which time he was credited with ten victories. He was awarded the Knight's Cross on 5 October 1941 following his 30th victory. Hohagen was subsequently wounded over Russia on numerous occasions, and returned to the West later in the war to take command of 7./JG 2 and then, on 7 April 1943, I./JG 27, operating in the defence of the Reich. However, he was shot down by Allied fighters over northern France on 1 June 1943, bailing out wounded from his burning Bf 109.

Following a period of hospitalisation, Hohagen was back in action as *Kommandeur* of I./JG 2 on 19 August 1943. Following an air battle over the Western Front in the autumn of 1944, Hohagen had been forced to belly land his stricken fighter in a small field. Aircraft and pilot had ploughed into a bank, and Hohagen smashed his head on the aircraft's reflector sight. A surgeon had to later replace a piece of his skull with plastic and pull the skin back together because of the injuries he suffered in this crash-landing. Even so, as Steinhoff later recalled, 'the two halves of his face no longer quite matched'.

Supposedly recovered from his injury, Hohagen was posted to III./EJG 2 at Lechfeld in late 1944, where he began to convert onto the Me 262, prior to taking command of the embryonic III./JG 7. Still troubled by headaches, however, as a direct result of his many wounds, and thus considered unfit for service by the Staff of the *General der Jagdflieger* and the Personnel Office, Hohagen had been returned to hospital near Berlin, from where Galland and Steinhoff had plucked him for operations once again. Of his total of 55 victories gained from over 500 missions, 13 were four-engined bombers.

Troubled by wounds, Major Karl-Heinz Schnell joined JV 44 from JG 102, prior to which he had flown operationally as *Kommandeur* of III./JG 51 and subsequently served on the staff at the RLM coordinating the activities of the fighter schools. He had been awarded the Knight's Cross in August 1941 in recognition of his 29 victories

Major Erich Hohagen sits in the cockpit of an Me 262 of III./EJG 2. Awarded the Knight's Cross in October 1941, Hohagen was one of the *Jagdwaffe's* most experienced unit commanders, having flown several thousand hours on some 60 different types of aircraft and been credited with the destruction of 13 four-engined bombers. A veteran of the Channel battles of 1940, he later saw action over Russia and in the defence of the Reich. During this time he bailed out of his aircraft, suffered serious wounds, flew more than 500 combat sorties and claimed 55 aerial victories. Hohagen suffered a bad head injury whilst flying as *Kommandeur* of I./JG 2 in the West in the autumn of 1944, and the aftereffects troubled him for the rest of his service career. He was one of the first pilots to join JV 44, and would later briefly serve as the unit's Technical Officer

Steinhoff also welcomed his former adjutant and wingman from his days with JG 77 in Italy, Leutnant Gottfried Fährmann. Fährmann had been shot down in combat by a P-38 over Yugoslavia on 10 May 1944, but gained revenge when he destroyed a Lightning 16 days later. The following month he claimed a P-51 shot down over Italy, but in July he was forced to bail out of his Bf 109 when it was hit by return fire from a B-25 Mitchell.

Representative of the valuable operational experience that Galland was now gathering around him was Unteroffizier Johann-Karl 'Jonny' Müller, an experienced ground-attack flier. Like Hohagen and Schnell, Müller had been hospitalised since mid-October 1944 until late January 1945 as a result of wounds incurred whilst flying Fw 190 *Jabos* in the East with II./SG 10. Müller had joined this unit in Normandy shortly after its formation as IV./SKG 10 in April 1943, and took part in a series of low-level 'nuisance' raids along the southeastern coast of England. Whilst engaged on these operations, Müller crash-landed his Fw 190 on at least two occasions in France, but was able to walk away unharmed. Later, in 1943, he saw action over Sicily and Italy until October of that year, when IV./SKG 10 was redesignated II./SG 10. By December 1943 the *Gruppe* had transferred to southern Russia.

Müller was wounded in mid-October 1944 whilst flying an escort mission for Stuka units repulsing the Soviet advance through Hungary – he had been flying these hazardous missions since the early autumn. Having recovered from his wounds, Müller found himself ordered to report to JV 44 at Brandenburg-Briest on 3 March 1945.

From the *Fluglehrerschule der Luftwaffe* (the central flying instructor's school) came a Leutnant Blomert, the former Ju 88 bomber pilot now specialising in blind-flying and navigational training using the Siebel Si 204. On 11 March fellow *Fluglehrerschule* instructor Feldwebel Otto Kammerdiener joined JV 44, having served with the formation leader's school at Quedlinburg since August 1944. Both would bring experience of twin-engine aircraft and asymmetric flying which would be a key element in the training of pilots converting to the Me 262.

Blomert and Kammerdiener joined the curious core assortment of unwanted *Experten* and *Ritterkreuzträger* (Knight's Cross holders) assembling at Brandenburg-Briest, along with a growing crop of virtually redundant fighter instructors from the operational training units JG 101, JG 102, JG 103 and JG 105. Many of the latter were combat-experienced pilots whose former fighter training units were all but disbanded, and whom Galland had been able to secure for JV 44 with the assistance of Trautloft and Schnell.

From JG 101 came Oberfeldwebel Leopold Knier. Earlier in the war, he had flown with II./JG 5 in the Far North, providing escort to bombers striking at Murmansk. On one such operation on 19 July 1942, Knier was bounced by Russian P-40s and his Bf 109 was hit. Bailing out, he landed behind enemy lines and was captured. Miraculously, however, he arrived back at his unit eight days later unharmed, and having, apparently, been made an offer by the Russians to 'kidnap' a Bf 109 and fly it to Murmansk for Soviet inspection in return for a large sum of money!

As strange as this story may seem, a similar offer was known to have been made to at least one other JG 5 pilot by the Russians operating in this

Unteroffizier Johann-Karl Müller joined JV 44 from II./SG 10 with the reputation of being a tenacious, low-level ground-attack pilot. He had seen action in the Mediterranean, the West and Russia, where he had been wounded flying Fw 190s with the *Schlacht* unit

Feldwebel Otto Kammerdiener was one of several instructor pilots who joined JV 44 at Brandenburg-Briest in mid-March 1945. A native of Hamburg, he would go on to claim at least one aerial victory whilst flying the Me 262 with the *Verband*

isolated theatre of war. Knier was later transferred to JG 101, before moving to Lechfeld to embark on Me 262 conversion with III./EJG 2. His assignment to JV 44 followed in March 1945.

From JG 103 came a 26-year-old instructor from Carinthia, Oberfeldwebel Josef 'Jupp' Dobnig, together with his fellow instructor and friend, Oberfeldwebel Siegfried 'Sigi' Schwaneberg. Dobnig had flown a total of 141 missions in the Bf 109 in Russia with II./JG 51, and then later in the Fw 190 with JG 26 in France, and was credited with nine victories. Posted to JG 103 in 1944, he was based initially at Stolp-Reitz, but the Russian advance later that year forced the *Geschwader* to make a transfer west to Wesendorf, where Dobnig managed to land in thick cloud on his last drops of fuel and his red fuel warning lamp blinking ominously. 'It was pure chaos', he recalled, 'Female Luftwaffe auxiliaries, Hungarian pilots, German pilots, Hitler Youth all crowded in'.

The order for him and Schwaneberg to report to JV 44 had come suddenly and very unexpectedly in early March, and it had saved them from training on the *Panzerfaust* anti-tank weapon which they – and

Oberfeldwebel Josef Dobnig joined JV 44 as an instructor from JG 103, before which he had served with II./JG 51 in Russia and JG 26 in France. 'Jupp' Dobnig would fly the Me 262 with JV 44. This portrait was taken while he was serving with the latter unit at Munich-Riem in March 1945

Former instructor pilot Oberfeldwebel Rudolf Nielinger, photographed at Munich-Riem whilst with JV 44. A veteran of Russia and North Africa, where he had flown with II./JG 51, he joined Galland's *Verband* from JG 103 on the Baltic coast, having supervised replacement pilots training up on the Bf 109 and Fw 190. Taken ill in North Africa in May 1943, by then Nielinger had 20 victories to his credit

Bavarian Unteroffizier Eduard Schallmoser was among the original cadre of pilots to join JV 44 at Brandenburg-Briest. Following a period of jet training with III./EJG 2 in late 1944 and early 1945, he would find himself defending the skies over his home in an Me 262 – with quite violent consequences

the rest of their cadre of student pilots at JG 103 – were expected to use as hurriedly trained 'infantry' against the envisaged approach of Soviet armour.

'At first we were speechless', remembered Dobnig, 'because this was Adolf Galland's elite unit. We'd heard that the Knight's Cross was virtually a part of their uniform. And now we two simple soldiers were to go there. But it was a much better prospect than fighting enemy tanks'.

Climbing aboard a train, Dobnig and Schwaneberg journeyed to Brandenburg-Briest, and when they reached the airfield, they discovered they were among the very first NCO pilots to report for operations with the new *Jagdverband*.

Also arriving from JG 103 was Oberfeldwebel Rudolf Nielinger, who had flown with II./JG 51 over France and Russia in 1941. Whilst flying the Bf 109 in a series of almost non-stop patrols in support of Army Group Centre's drive on Moscow, he had accumulated his first nine victories.

In early November 1942, having survived 280 missions over Russia, Nielinger was transferred, along with the rest of II./JG 51 (under the command of Hauptmann Hartmann Grasser), to Tunisia as reinforcement intended to engage Allied fighters covering the enemy advances following the Allied landings in French Morocco and Algeria. Success came quickly to Rudolf Nielinger in Tunisia, and he scored his first victory when he downed a Bristol Beaufort northwest of Bizerte only three days after arriving in Africa. He would not score again for six months.

Nielinger eventually found himself pitted against British bombers escorted by droves of Spitfires as the Eighth Army pushed against the Mareth Line in March 1943. On 20 April II./JG 51 fled for Sicily, and in May it moved again, this time to Sardinia, where Nielinger scored his 20th, and final, victory (a Curtiss P-40), before leaving the island in September for a brief sojourn in the Reich. In January 1944 he rejoined his *Gruppe* in Italy, where it was now flying ground-attack escort missions over the Anzio beach head, but at the end of that month Nielinger was taken seriously ill, probably as a result of his service in Africa, and once again returned to Germany.

Following a period of recuperation, Nielinger was assigned as an instructor at the fighter training wing JG 103, based on the Baltic coast. Here, his responsibilities were to train desperately needed fighter pilots in the tried and tested *Rotte* and *Schwarm* formations using an assortment of ageing Bf 109Es as well as the more modern Fw 190.

However, by early 1945 the majority of the A/B and C training schools were being disbanded, and thus the need for instructors had diminished considerably. Nevertheless, these pilots had been trained to instruct on blind flying and in instrument courses, and were thus ideal for JV 44's needs. So it was that Oberfeldwebel Nielinger received orders to report to Galland, and he arrived at Brandenburg-Briest in an Fw 190 on 11 March 1945, where he was surprised to find that he was to go operational on the Me 262!

JV 44 did count amongst its ranks at this time at least one pilot who had been fully trained to fly the jet fighter. In late November 1944, former night-flying instructor Unteroffizier Eduard Schallmoser was posted to 9./EJG 2 at Landsberg to begin preparatory training for the Me 262A-1a standard fighter. With 'faultless' take-off and landing skills, good flying capability, confidence and reasonable gunnery, Schallmoser had been recommended by his previous commanding officer at 12./EJG 1 for jet fighter training. This involved four-and-a-half hours spent practising on the twin-engined Si 204 and Bf 110, with a further six hours on a Bü 181 for gunnery and target skills.

On 10 January 1945 Schallmoser moved to Unterschlauersbach for final conversion to the Me 262 with 10./EJG 2. As with his earlier training, his instructor at Lechfeld was very satisfied with his abilities, and upon the successful completion of his conversion training, Schallmoser received his posting to JV 44 on 2 March 1945. The next day he travelled to Brandenburg-Briest.

Together, Galland, Steinhoff, Blomert and Kammerdiener forged ahead with the necessarily hurried and rudimentary training of their pilots. From the *Fluglehrerschule der Luftwaffe*, Galland had secured the services of a small number of Si 204s, these sturdy aircraft proving ideal for teaching pilots the art of twin-engine take-offs and landings, instruction on the the *Zielvorsatzgerät* 16 radio course indicator, general navigation, instrument flying and single-engine flying. At least three Siebels are known to have been on the strength of JV 44 at this time.

Between 4 and 18 March, Blomert sought to give the unit's small group of pilots a crash training course in twin-engine flying and navigational techniques. Flights were made in Siebels from Briest, with aircraft heading north to Greifswald, via Oranienburg, and to Burg and Goslar.

By 14 March 1945, JV 44 had taken delivery of its first Me 262s. Erich Hohagen recalled;

'I had only received one week's training on the Me 262 at Lechfeld as far as I remember, but I was very proud and honoured to fly it since I was still suffering from a head fracture that had occurred one month before. It was the absolute fulfilment of my flying career, and I knew for sure that, at that

Playing a key role in the training of JV 44's cadre of former single-engined instructor pilots on to the twin-engined Me 262 were the unit's Siebel Si 204s, one of which is seen here at Munich-Riem in May 1945. It is believed that these aircraft had previously been on the strength of the *Fluglehrerschule der Luftwaffe*, which had been operating at Brandenburg-Briest in February 1945

time, no further enhancements could be made. It was the biggest step since the Wright brothers flew an aircraft heavier than air.

'Basically, with the Me 262, its flight characteristics bore no similarity to other aircraft that I had flown, and although it was easier to handle from a piloting perspective, things were much more critical from a flight safety point of view. For example, the engines could have been improved and better fatigue resistance built in. I also felt that the hydraulic system was insufficient, and that the aircraft would have benefited from the installation of dive brakes.'

Feldwebel Franz Steiner, an experienced fighter pilot who had joined JV 44 from JG 11, remembered;

'I was selected by *Generalleutnant* Galland in person after a short conversation with him. Exactly what criteria I had to make him want to hang on to me and send others away, I don't know. For me, the most important thing was to fly the "legendary bird". Conversion onto the Me 262 at Brandenburg-Briest didn't give me any problems. Steinhoff just gave me a few prior instructions and then told me to take off on my first flight!

'I have to say that flying the Me 262 was the high point in my flying career. Whenever you first got off the ground and had attained height and

Feldwebel Franz Steiner, photographed here as a member of I./JG 11 on Reich defence duties in Germany during 1944. Steiner was an accomplished fighter pilot who was credited with the destruction of nine four-engined bombers. He never knew why he was selected by Galland to join JV 44, but the transfer suited Steiner fine, as his main desire was to fly the Me 262

speed, you couldn't help but feel a sense of absolute elation and wonderment. In my view, the only weak point was the engines. Engine failure during take-off, which, unfortunately, was all too common, almost always meant certain death for a pilot. You would have felt safer with rocket-assisted take-off. In flight, especially in a shallow dive, you had to adjust for the sensitivity of the engines too much.'

Described as 'a passionate flier', Steiner had flown with JG 27 from the summer of 1940, serving in the Balkans and North Africa. Posted back to Europe in early 1942, he joined 8./JG 1 and was almost immediately moved to Trondheim, in Norway, as part of *Kommando Losigkeit*. This unit, manned by pilots from JG 1, was intended to offer air protection to vessels of the *Kriegsmarine* seeking shelter along the Norwegian coast and in the fjords following the 'Channel Dash' from France.

Steiner continued his duties with JG 1 until mid-1944, when he spent a brief spell as a fighter instructor with an *Ergänzungsgruppe* in Märkisch-Friedland. He then joined 2./JG 11, flying Fw 190s over the homeland and claiming five B-17s, four B-24s, a P-38 and a B-26 shot down.

JV 44's 'training programme' – such as it was – continued into late March, and suffered little from the effects of Allied bombing, although the small town of Brandenburg was bombed at least once during the unit's tenure at Briest. Fuel was also available in reasonable supply, but needed careful supervision, and training flights often doubled up as patrols with aircraft fully-armed, their pilots briefed to shoot down any enemy aircraft they might encounter.

Josef Dobnig remembers his initial training, which was supervised by Steinhoff;

'Within a few days of leaving JG 103 at Wesendorf, "Sigi" Schwaneberg and I were at JV 44 receiving our training on the Me 262, which,

A rare view of pilots of JV 44 gathered outside airfield buildings at Brandenburg-Briest in March 1945 during the unit's preparatory phase. They are, from left to right, Unteroffizier Eduard Schallmoser, Feldwebel Otto Kammerdiener, Oberfeldwebel Josef Dobnig, Feldwebel Franz Steiner, (unidentified), (unidentified), Oberfeldwebel Leopold Knier, (unidentified) and Oberleutnant Blomert. Why most of the men are wearing civilian clothes is unknown

According to first-hand accounts and photographic evidence, as well as a surviving log book entry, at least one two-seat training variant of the Messerschmitt jet fighter (Me 262B-1a 'White S') was available to the fledgling jet pilots of JV 44 at Brandenburg-Briest in March 1945. However, flying time allocated to individual pilots was extremely limited. Seen here in the foreground surrounded by other abandoned airframes at Munich-Riem, 'White S' was eventually scrapped shortly after VE-Day

In mid-March 1945, Generalmajor Josef Kammhuber, the former head of the Luftwaffe nightfighter force, was appointed Göring's General Plenipotentiary for Jet Aircraft, and in such capacity, he ordered JV 44 to become operational as soon as possible

aeronautically, was a completely new challenge. At first we were given a single familiarisation flight in a two-seat aircraft. But there was neither time nor sufficient fuel for a really good grounding on the type.'

In fact Dobnig recalls that Steinhoff directly oversaw his training, and his log book testifies that the ace accompanied him on four flights in a Si 204 to familiarise him with a twin-engined type in readiness for the Me 262. Furthermore, blind-flying training was given by closing curtains over the cockpit panels and conducting simulated flying on instruments.

On 18 March, Unteroffizier Dobnig flew an Me 262 solo for the first time over Brandenburg, less than two weeks after arriving at JV 44. That same day Generalmajor Josef Kammhuber, who at the beginning of the year had been appointed the *Generalbevollmächtiger des Reichsmarschalls für Strahlfluzeuge* (the General Plenipotentiary of the Reichsmarschall for Jet Aircraft), ordered *'Jagdverband 44 General Galland'* to be operational as soon as possible with a strength of 20 aircraft.

Before the end of the month two more veteran *Jagdflieger* joined JV 44 – apparently because of disciplinary issues. Fahnen-junker Oberfeldwebel Klaus Neumann, who had received a Knight's Cross four months earlier for his performance in bringing down no fewer than 19 American four-engined bombers, had begun his operational career with 2./JG 51 in Russia in May 1943. Having been credited with 12 victories while on the Eastern Front, Neumann returned with his *Staffel* to Germany in late June 1944.

Neumann's unit was was redesignated 16./JG 3 in August and assigned to IV.(*Sturm*)/JG 3. Now tasked with knocking down USAAF heavy bombers, Neumann proved to be a lethal exponent of this dangerous art. On 25 November, he was awarded the Knight's Cross in recognition for the shooting down of his 19th *'Viermot'*, and it was presented to him 'officially' by Hitler on 9 December 1944.

In January 1945, the young *Experte* was transferred to a staff position with JG 7, but it was here that he clashed with Theo Weissenberger, the unit's recently appointed *Kommodore*. 'Weissenberger had just taken over from Steinhoff', Neumann recalled, 'and I got into trouble with him – it was for personal reasons. Shortly afterwards, Steinhoff and then Galland approached me and asked me if I wanted to join their new unit. I could see no problem with that, so I went along and just got on with the job'.

Franz Stigler had flown 480 combat missions with II./JG 27 over Africa, Sicily, Italy and the homeland. He had shot down 28 enemy aircraft flying the Bf 109, scoring 17 of his kills over North Africa, with a further five claimed against four-engined bombers over Italy and Austria. Stigler had been shot down on no fewer than 17 occasions, from which he had bailed out six times! In early 1945 he was posted to III./EJG 2 at Lechfeld for eight weeks to undergo conversion onto the Me 262. Stigler remembered;

'I finished my training at Lechfeld having flown the Me 262 just once. I then moved to EJG 1 for a short spell. The training in the unit was very rudimentary, and I made a stupid remark about it and was ordered to leave. In the meantime, word had got out that Galland was forming a new jet unit at Brandenburg, so I called him from Lechfeld and asked whether I could join him – after all, I had just been trained to fly the Me 262. He said, "Sure, just bring a jet with you"! So I went over to the jet production plant at Leipheim and tried to get hold of an Me 262. I said I was under instruction to collect the aircraft for JV 44, but they had never even heard of the unit.

'Anyway, by that stage, things were in such turmoil that I managed to secure the aircraft, and I then flew direct to Brandenburg-Briest. I didn't do much when I got there though because the unit was in the process of getting organised, and we were left well alone. However, it was good to run into my old squadronmate from Africa, Rudi Sinner, who was now with JG 7.'

Soon Galland was trying out new tactics with the Me 262. On 22 March he personally led a flight of three jets out from Briest to test the aircraft's performance in a *Kette*, as opposed to the conventional four-aircraft *Schwarm* made up of a pair of *Rotten* favoured by JG 7.

Over the next few days comparison flights followed in flights of four, led by Galland and Steinhoff, who were accompanied variously by Schallmoser, Nielinger, Kammerdiener and Steiner. Galland and Steinhoff had observed that the large turning radius and slow acceleration of the Me 262 made the *Kette* element of three aircraft more versatile. The *Kette* later became preferred by JV 44 due to the Me 262's lack of manoeuvrability, which made maintaining formation in a larger element extremely difficult. As Galland recalled;

'The *Kette* appealed to us because on our runways, which were all 60 metres wide, three aircraft could take off side-by-side simultaneously, whereas a fourth aircraft couldn't have gotten onto the runway and would have had to have taken off later after quite an interval of time. It would then have had the difficulty of establishing contact with the rest of the formation. Therefore, we reverted to the *Kette*, and flew this way with slightly less intermediate spacing than we would have flown with conventionally engined aircraft – about 100 metres apart when climbing, and thereafter about 150-180 metres in level flight. These reduced intervals made it easier for the formation to keep together.

'Assembling after take-off only works providing the following aircraft takes off very quickly afterwards – a thing which is not so easy for jet fighters owing to their unwieldiness on the ground. In the *Kette*, aircraft are generally staggered below or behind each other, but not above each other owing to the range of vision of the Me 262 – when passing above,

Leutnant Klaus Neumann had been awarded the Knight's Cross by Hitler in December 1944 for his operations against US daylight heavy bombers. While flying with IV.(*Sturm*)/JG 3, he was accredited with 17 'Viermots' shot down. He later transferred to JV 44 from JG 7 in March 1945, having suffered disagreements with the *Kommodore* of the latter unit, Major Theo Weissenberger

Oberleutnant Franz Stigler had seen combat in North Africa and the Mediterranean with II./JG 27. Shot down no fewer than 17 times, he had nevertheless flown nearly 500 combat sorties and had 28 aerial victories to his credit, including five four-engined bombers. In early 1945 Stigler was assigned to train up on the Me 262 with III./EJG 2, but within weeks he would find himself with JV 44 flying combat missions in the jet fighter over Bavaria

you lost sight of the leading aircraft, and it could be difficult to find it again. Only when diving, when putting the nose down steeply, could a formation leader let the rest of the formation know his intentions. In such a case, one could then pass overhead and bank in.'

It was a *Kette* of Me 262s which Steinhoff led, accompanied by Klaus Neumann and Leutnant Blomert, on what is believed to have been the first combat operation mounted by JV 44 some time in the last days of March. Banking around the Plauer See just south of Briest shortly after take-off, the three jets made course over Berlin and then to the east, following the course of the road towards Frankfurt an der Oder. Approaching the Oder and the frontlines, the Me 262s flew into light flak and then descended so as to assess the situation on the ground.

Turning for home a little later, the jets suddenly encountered a loose formation of Soviet fighters over the river. The German pilots found themselves momentarily uncertain as to how best to take on the ragged and lumbering enemy fighters in their high-speed interceptors. Steinhoff rolled his Me 262 over, and as he did so, he observed a formation of Il-2s strafing a German transport column a short distance away. He recorded;

'As I bent forward to look through the sight, I noticed that I had too much speed again. The trees and fields were flashing past beneath me and the shape of the last fighter-bomber loomed alarmingly in the sight. The burst of fire was very short. The *Shturmovik* started leaving a trail just as I pulled up over it, the tips of the tall pines almost seeming to brush the Me 262's wings. The fighter-bomber hit the ground not far from the edge of the forest, first with its airscrew, then bouncing along on its belly, throwing up a gigantic fountain of powdery snow. Blomert was still having trouble keeping up and on the way back he told me he was running short of fuel. We reached Brandenburg on the last of our reserve.'

On another occasion in late March 1945, Oberfeldwebel Dobnig was forced to make an emergency landing in his Me 262 after taking off on

One of the first Me 262s to be assigned to JV 44 was 'Red S', photographed here at Brandenburg-Briest in March 1945. It was used for conversion and familiarisation purposes by Müller, Nielinger, Dobnig and Steiner

One of JV 44's Me 262s is prepared for a sortie at Brandenburg-Briest under the curious gaze of airfield staff and civilian officials

what would be his first – yet abortive – combat mission when sent aloft to intercept incoming enemy bombers approaching Hamburg. Over Stendal, having been airborne for only a short while, he experienced a severe malfunction in the fuel system, which had, unbeknown to him, been leaking, and he came down with his tanks virtually empty near a hamlet northwest of Stendal. The hamlet had no police station at which he could register his presence, so Dobnig walked into the tiny post office, from where the post mistress allowed him to call his airfield. He was collected that night by car and returned to Briest.

Meanwhile, *General der Flieger* Koller issued orders for JV 44 to relocate to southern Germany in order to operate in the defence of the aircraft manufacturing plants and fuel and ammunition storage facilities in the area which were being targeted relentlessly by Allied bombers. Adolf Galland decided to leave Briest and drive south alone in his BMW sports car so that he could hastily reconnoitre potential landing grounds in Bavaria. One of his first stops was at Lechfeld, where he endeavoured, unsuccessfully, to recruit Erich Hartmann into his unit. Hartmann, the highest-scoring fighter pilot in the world, declined Galland's request and returned to JG 52, which was operating in the defence of Czechoslovakia.

Galland eventually arrived at Munich-Riem, a major civil airport located nine kilometres east of Munich between the villages of Riem and Feldkirchen. Designed by *Prof. Dr.-Ing.* Ernst Sagebiel, the architect who had created the state-of-the-art aerodromes at Berlin-Tempelhof and Stuttgart-Echterdingen, Riem had seen considerable redevelopment since the 1930s. Indeed, it featured a new departures hall, technical site, workshops and electrical and optical equipment for night landing.

The airport shared the same oval-shaped design which Sagebiel had established at Tempelhof and Echterdingen. Both the departure and arrival halls, as well as the control tower, were contained in one vast, continuously curving structure located close to the northern perimeter,

This panoramic view of a battered and bombed-out Munich-Riem airport in June 1945 shows its vast buildings and control tower. Lined up in front of the badly damaged passenger terminal is a varied collection of abandoned Luftwaffe aircraft, including two Si 204s, an Me 262 and an Fw 190D-9, all of which were probably aircraft of JV 44

whilst to either side of this building were various workshops and stores. The airfield boasted a well drained grass surface. The east-west axis measured just over 2000 metres and the north-south axis spanned just over 1500 metres. Two broad starting platforms made of concrete lay at each end of the east-west axis, each one measuring some 320 metres.

The new airport had opened officially on 1 September 1939, and in October of that year, the trans-Alpine Berlin-Stuttgart-Venice-Rome route was opened. Throughout the war, Riem operated as a transit point for a multitude of Luftwaffe units arriving from or going to the east and south, as well as a 'hub' for German airline *Deutsche Lufthansa* (DLH), which, from 1941, operated direct non-stop services from there to Berlin, Venice, Zurich and Lyon.

Later, in the winter of 1944, as a result of heavy Allied air attacks on the airfield at Stuttgart, DLH transferred its Ju 90-equipped Berlin (Stuttgart)-Barcelona-Madrid-Lisbon service to Riem, and this continued to operate through to the end of hostilities in May 1945. Additionally, DLH maintained large engine repair workshops there in which work was done for both its own machines and those of the Luftwaffe.

Importantly, the runway could accommodate the take-off distance of 1850 metres needed by an Me 262 with a full fuel load and ordnance. Galland was convinced it would make a good operational base. Climbing into the BMW, he motored back to Brandenburg and quickly began making arrangements for the transfer. He telephoned Generalmajor Kammhuber, who, as Göring's 'Plenipotentiary', would organise the required transport. Kammhuber must have moved quickly, for on 29 March a heavily laden freight train rolled out of Berlin carrying JV 44's groundcrews, vehicles, engine spares, signals equipment and flying gear bound for Munich.

However, despite Galland having mustered sufficient support personnel and equipment, he still lacked pilots and aircraft. As late as 31 March, the Luftwaffe operations staff recorded that just nine Me 262s had been delivered from the factories to JV 44, and one of these was undergoing repair – six more were unserviceable as a result of enemy air attacks on Brandenburg-Briest. Another two machines were expected to arrive from training units. By comparison, JG 7 reported 79 of its aircraft as serviceable that day.

Adverse weather over eastern and southern Germany had delayed transfer on the 30th. Then, on the 31st, as the weather cleared, and presumably with his aircraft having been hurriedly serviced, Galland arranged for half of his meagre force of 20 pilots to ferry the jets to Riem;

'We really had to speed things up in order to become operationally ready. Oberst Steinhoff was a pillar of strength to me, and he pursued preparations to become combat ready with considerable energy. The task of getting all the transports ready which would carry our crews was handled brilliantly.'

At dawn, Oberst Steinhoff took off with the first group, followed at 1740 hrs that afternoon by Fahnen-junker Oberfeldwebel Neumann leading the second. Behind the Me 262s came two of JV 44's Si 204 liaison aircraft piloted by Feldwebel Kammerdiener and Leutnant Blomert. The first carried more signals equipment, and Kammerdiener was accompanied by Leutnant Hoffmann, an Me 262 instructor who had just reported to JV 44 from III./EJG 2 at Lechfeld. The second Siebel carried Generalleutnant Galland, Unteroffizier Müller and Unteroffizier Schallmoser, who brought further equipment with them.

One by one, the jets touched down on the grass at Riem, flown in by Steinhoff, Hohagen, Stigler, Fährmann and Steiner. Oberfeldwebel Nielinger, flying Me 262 'White 7', suffered engine failure after flying some 540 km and made an emergency landing at Unterschlauersbach. Klaus Neumann accompanied him in, and while the mechanics fixed Nielinger's engine, the two JV 44 pilots used the opportunity to look over an Ar 234 jet bomber that had also landed there with engine trouble.

Eventually all the jets and the Siebels arrived, as did the contents of the train. *Jagdverband 44* began installing itself at its new base. By this stage of the war, Riem had been transformed to accommodate both Luftwaffe

Freshly arrived at Munich-Riem, the tall form of Unteroffizier Eduard Schallmoser in a forage cap is recognisable as he and another, unidentified pilot of JV 44 walk past Me 262 'White 5' Wk-Nr. 111745, with 'White 6' the next aircraft along. Note the primitive, and probably very inadequate, camouflage netting draped over the aircraft in an attempt at concealment from the air in the open space at Riem

aircraft and personnel. An underground fuel store had been constructed close to the largest of the two main hangars, the frontage of which spanned nearly 400 metres and the rear of which contained nine workshops. The second hangar measured nearly 130 metres, and was located next to the motor transport depot.

To the west of the large hangar, a four storey building contained administrative, meteorological, signals and medical offices. Airfield personnel were quartered in an extreme western section of the sprawling semi-circular building, originally designed by Sagebiel as a hotel for passengers. A compass swinging base was situated in front of the main hangar and ammunition storage pens were built close to the main Munich-Muhldorf road, from which was gained access to the airfield.

Aircraft could be sheltered in up to 35 large, purpose-built blast pens located off the north and south perimeter roads, although there was a large number of effectively abandoned aircraft of different types lying on the grass areas around the airport. Three heavy flak emplacements had been built for base defence to the southwest of the field, with 12 more for light flak batteries scattered to the north, east, south and west – what condition both these and the blast pens were in by April 1945 is questionable.

However, there would be little time for Galland's men to acquaint themselves with their surroundings. As soon as the Me 262s were pushed back into the blast pens, orders were issued to start digging one-man foxholes around the dispersal, ready for occupation at a moment's notice. At Riem, the threat was not just from Allied bombers but also lower level strafing attacks and bombing raids by American fighters and fighter-bombers. This was to be JV 44's home for the next month while engaged in operations against the American air forces over southern Germany.

Oberfeldwebel Leopold Knier of JV 44 looks on as fellow pilots and groundcrew push an Me 262 back towards the dispersal stand at Munich-Riem in early April 1945. The pilot in the leather flying suit and goggles to the right of the photograph is possibly Leutnant Gottfried Fährmann, formerly of JG 77, who had served as Oberst Steinhoff's wingman and adjutant in the Mediterranean

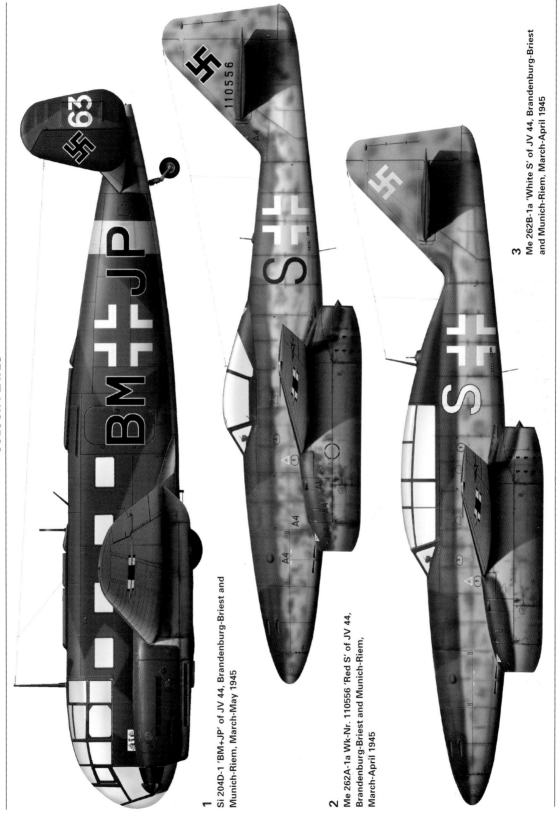

1
Si 204D-1 'BM+JP' of JV 44, Brandenburg-Briest and
Munich-Riem, March-May 1945

2
Me 262A-1a Wk-Nr. 110556 'Red S' of JV 44,
Brandenburg-Briest and Munich-Riem,
March-April 1945

3
Me 262B-1a 'White S' of JV 44, Brandenburg-Briest
and Munich-Riem, March-April 1945

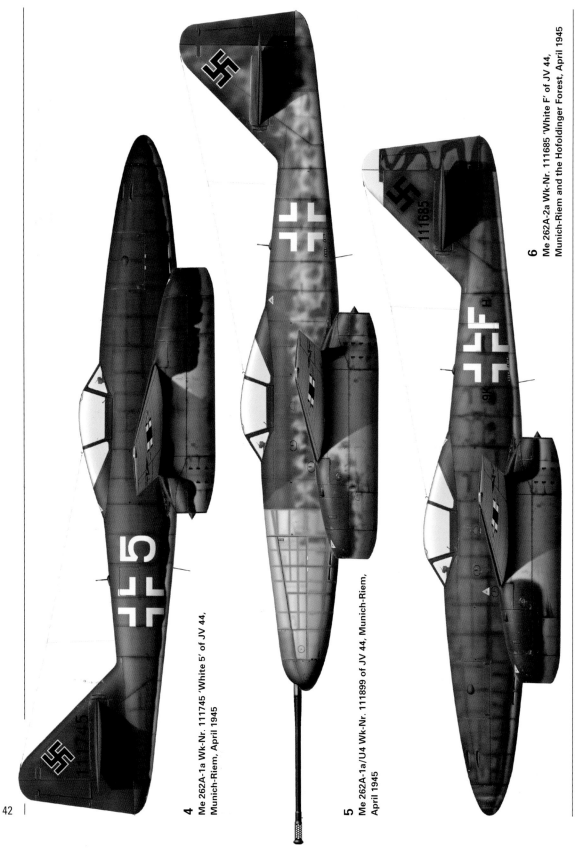

4
Me 262A-1a Wk-Nr. 111745 'White 5' of JV 44,
Munich-Riem, April 1945

5
Me 262A-1a/U4 Wk-Nr. 111899 of JV 44, Munich-Riem,
April 1945

6
Me 262A-2a Wk-Nr. 111685 'White F' of JV 44,
Munich-Riem and the Hofoldinger Forest, April 1945

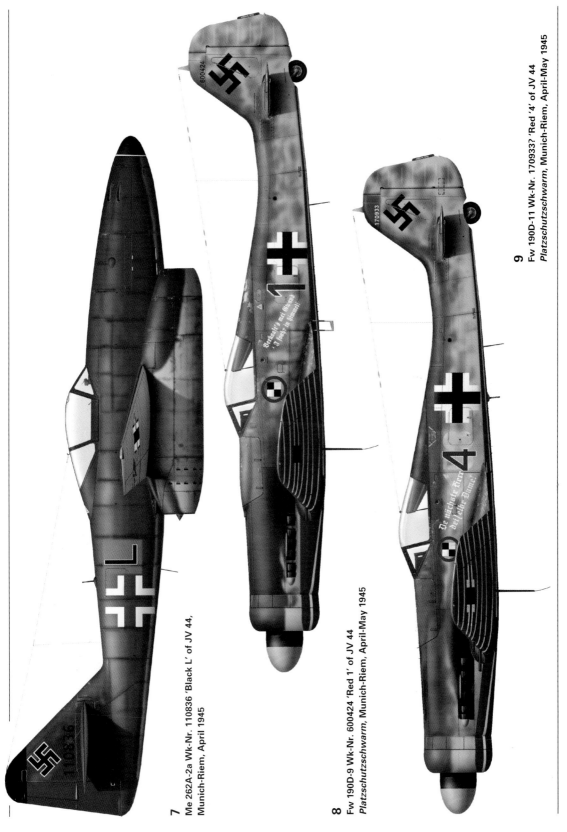

7
Me 262A-2a Wk-Nr. 110836 'Black L' of JV 44,
Munich-Riem, April 1945

8
Fw 190D-9 Wk-Nr. 600424 'Red 1' of JV 44
Platzschutzschwarm, Munich-Riem, April-May 1945

9
Fw 190D-11 Wk-Nr. 170933? 'Red '4' of JV 44
Platzschutzschwarm, Munich-Riem, April-May 1945

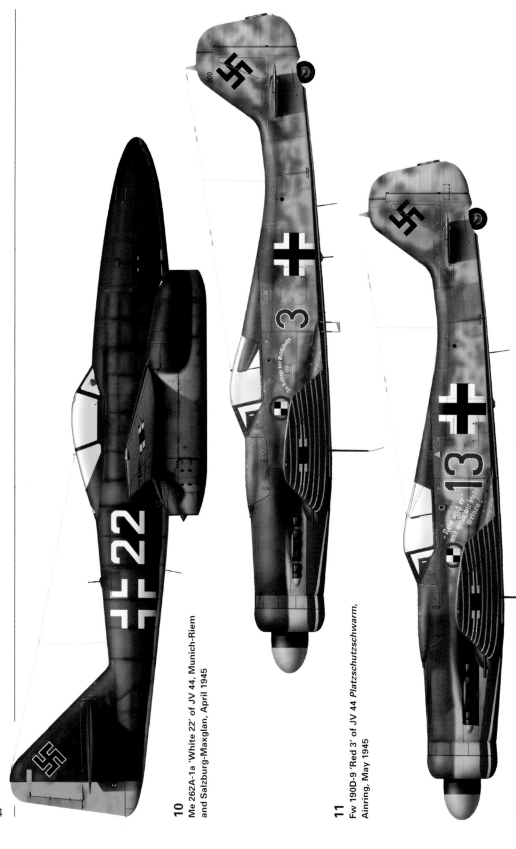

10
Me 262A-1a 'White 22' of JV 44, Munich-Riem
and Salzburg-Maxglan, April 1945

11
Fw 190D-9 'Red 3' of JV 44 *Platzschutzschwarm*,
Ainring, May 1945

12
Fw 190D-9 Wk-Nr. 213240 'Red 13' of JV 44
Platzschutzschwarm, Ainring, May 1945

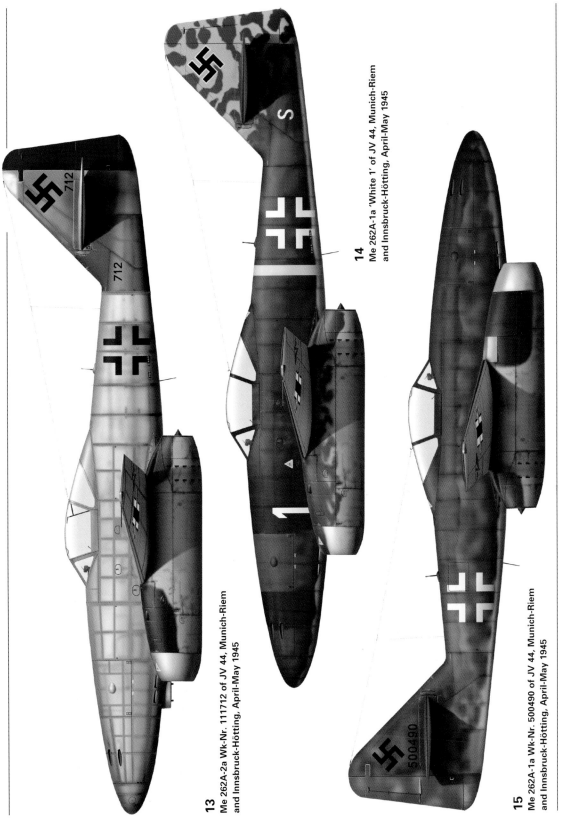

13
Me 262A-2a Wk-Nr. 111712 of JV 44, Munich-Riem and Innsbruck-Hötting, April-May 1945

14
Me 262A-1a 'White 1' of JV 44, Munich-Riem and Innsbruck-Hötting, April-May 1945

15
Me 262A-1a Wk-Nr. 500490 of JV 44, Munich-Riem and Innsbruck-Hötting, April-May 1945

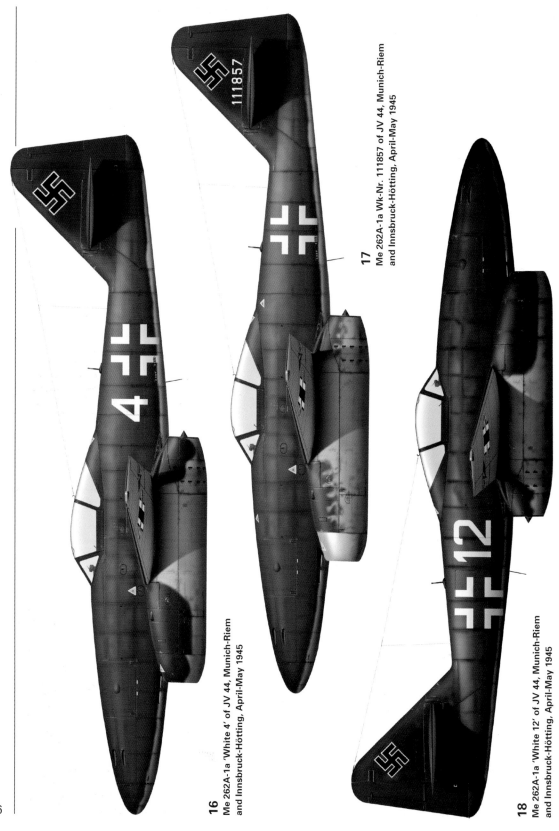

16
Me 262A-1a 'White 4' of JV 44, Munich-Riem
and Innsbruck-Hötting, April-May 1945

17
Me 262A-1a Wk-Nr. 111857 of JV 44, Munich-Riem
and Innsbruck-Hötting, April-May 1945

18
Me 262A-1a 'White 12' of JV 44, Munich-Riem
and Innsbruck-Hötting, April-May 1945

BATS OUT OF HELL

Throughout March 1945, the US Eighth, Twelfth and Fifteenth Air Forces continued their relentless and punishing bombing campaign against aircraft and tank factories, oil refineries, railways, road junctions, ammunition dumps and bridges across southern Germany, Austria and Czechoslovakia. On the 25th – just one week before JV 44 arrived at Munich-Riem – more than 150 B-24 Liberators of the Fifteenth Air Force bombed the jet aircraft production facility at Neuberg, while other heavy bombers struck at airfields at Erding, Munich and Plattling.

On the 31st, the fighter groups of the Fifteenth enjoyed their highest-scoring day of the year, claiming no fewer than 35 German fighters shot down over the area. The pressure on the German civilian and military infrastructure was immense. Worse was to come.

While his unit prepared itself for imminent operations against the bombers, Galland doggedly sought out new pilots. He had received word that Hauptmann Walter Krupinski was 'resting' at a recuperation centre for wounded and mentally strained Luftwaffe aircrew known as 'Florida' at Bad Wiessee, to the south of Munich on the Tegernsee. He had been there for less than a week when he received two surprise visitors who made him an offer that he could not refuse;

'It would have been the night of 1 April 1945. Steinhoff and Galland turned up completely unexpectedly at the recreation centre. I thought they were still up in the north at Brandenburg-Briest – I'd heard about this

Taken just before or after a flight, Oberst Johannes Steinhoff appears to cast a somewhat anxious glance over his shoulder in this photograph, taken at Munich-Riem. To the right, wearing sunglasses, is Leutnant Gottfried Fährmann

The rambling orphanage at Feldkirchen which served as JV 44's main headquarters and also provided its personnel with their accommodation in April 1945

unit Galland had formed. In fact they had flown their aircraft down to München-Riem that day and had come straight to Bad Wiessee. Steinhoff asked me if I wanted to fly the Me 262. I was astonished, but immediately said "Yes!"'

With its officer cadre of Steinhoff, Krupinski, Schnell, Hohagen, Fährmann, Stigler and Neumann, backed up by experienced Unteroffizier and NCOs such as Nielinger, Schallmoser, Müller, Steiner, Dobnig, Knier and Kammerdiener, JV 44 was building a strong core of capable and experienced pilots. While Galland set up his personal quarters

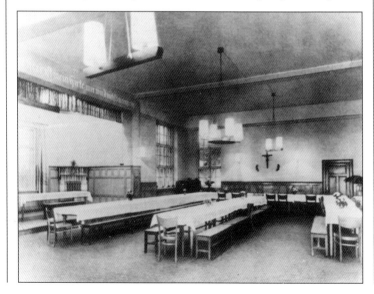

A view of the main dining room of the orphanage in which the pilots of JV 44 took their meals. Galland would sit with his men at one end of the long tables to be served by orderlies, while belts and pistols were hung on the wall. Josef Dobnig remembered the room as being 'gloomy'

in a local forester's lodge, his pilots accommodated themselves in the villages around Riem and established a battle headquarters, or *Gefechtsstand*, in a former orphanage at Feldkirchen, three kilometres south of the airport, which also had enough space to house an operations room, stores, accommodation and vehicle shelter.

Josef Dobnig, one of the original cadre of instructor pilots who joined JV 44 at Brandenburg-Briest, recalled communal meals taken over a very long table in a large, somewhat gloomy dining room at Feldkirchen with great doors that opened out on to lawns. Pilots would hang their belts and pistols over coat hooks fitted to the wall, before taking their seat to dine. Breakfasts were a casual affair, but evening meals were arranged according to a formal seating plan, with Galland and his staff sitting along one side of the table – with Galland at the centre – while the pilots sat opposite. Food and drink was served by specially assigned orderlies.

Galland next appointed an adjutant for his unit. He chose Hauptmann Werner Gutowski, once a protégé of Steinhoff, who subsequently served on his fighter staff. A veteran of the Channel battles of 1940, Gutowski had flown with the *Geschwaderstab* JG 77 in Italy and III./JG 11, before being transferred to the *Stab General der Jagdflieger*. After Galland's dismissal, however, he found relations with Gollob strained and readily accepted Galland's offer of a position with JV 44 at Riem.

Arriving from Berlin, Gutowski quickly set up the operations room at Feldkirchen. Soon, one of the great, high-ceilinged rooms of the orphanage was fitted with an enormous glass panel, beneath which was a detailed map of southern Germany and Austria that Gutowski would plot the *Verband's* operations and enemy incursions on. The surface of the glass was divided into a grid of squares stretching from Munich to Augsburg, Regensburg and Nuremberg, with each city labelled in red crayon.

Over the following days, more pilots reported for duty. Hauptmann Rüdiger von Kirchmayr joined JV 44 at this time, having been awarded the Knight's Cross the previous month for his impressive record against four-engined bombers in the defence of the Reich (although the first recommendation for this award to him had been rejected). This 23-year-old

Hauptmann Werner Gutowski was an experienced fighter pilot who had served with 1. Erg.Gr./JG 52 and been *Staffelkapitän* of 9./JG 1, prior to being transferred to *Stab*/JG 77. He was selected by Galland to manage JV 44's operations room at Feldkirchen

Hauptmann Rüdiger von Kirchmayr, seen here as a Leutnant while with 4./JG 1 at Woensdrecht in June 1942, joined JV 44 in April 1945. Awarded the Knight's Cross in March 1945, this Austrian *Jagdflieger* had been particularly successful in operations against four-engined bombers. Unfortunately, little is known about his service with JV 44

Austrian had taken over as acting *Kommandeur* of II./JG 1 for a month in the summer of 1944, before being appointed *Kapitän* of 5./JG 1.

On 11 August 1944, von Kirchmayr had suffered a head injury when his Fw 190 was attacked by a P-51 in France while making a landing. On 19 September he was posted to the *Stab*/JG 11 and then assumed command of I./JG 11 on 25 November, which he led until his posting to JV 44. By war's end, von Kirchmayr had flown nearly 400 missions and had been accredited with 46 victories, including as many as 20 four-engined bomber kills.

Oberleutnant Karl-Heinz Schrader, who was the last *Staffelkapitän* of the disbanded 12./JG 26, had followed his erstwhile *Kommandeur*, Walter Krupinski, from 'Florida' to JV 44 – but his stay with the unit would not last long.

Like Krupinski, Knight's Cross-holder Oberfeldwebel Herbert Kaiser had been coaxed out of 'Florida'. Kaiser was a veteran NCO pilot with combat experience gained from nearly 1000 missions flown on virtually every front, and whose operational career had commenced in 1938 when he flew under the command of a young Johannes Steinhoff in 2./JG 132 at Jever. From there he spent a brief time flying Bf 109Bs with *Trägergruppe* 186 which was being prepared as a carrier-based fighter group in readiness for the completion of the *Kriegsmarine's* aircraft carrier, the *Graf Zeppelin*.

However, when this project was scrapped in 1939, the *Gruppe* was integrated into III./JG 77, with which Kaiser flew Bf 109s successively in the invasion of Poland, the West, Rumania, Greece and Russia.

Oberfeldwebel Herbert Kaiser joined JV 44 after a long period of hospitalisation following wounds suffered in air combat over France with III./JG 1. For a time, he was assigned to coordinate JV 44's aircraft movements on the ground at Riem

In October 1942, III./JG 77 was sent to North Africa, where Kaiser shot down five enemy aircraft but was badly wounded. A short spell as a fighter instructor in the south of France followed in January 1943, as well as the award of the Knight's Cross, but Kaiser was soon reunited with III./JG 77 for the defence of Sardinia and Italy, where he shot down another four enemy machines.

In January 1944 Kaiser was transferred yet again when he received orders to join III./JG 1. He fought in Normandy, but on 6 August his Bf 109 was attacked over Paris by a Spitfire escorting a formation of RAF Lancasters. Although Kaiser managed to escape his burning fighter by bailing out, his right leg became entangled in his parachute shroud and he collided with the rudder. Suffering from multiple fractures to the right thigh, he was hospitalised in France and then Germany until the end of February 1945, when he was transferred to Bad Wiessee to await a posting. Kaiser was 29 years old and had scored 68 victories, but as a result of the severity of his wounds, flying an aircraft such as the Me 262 was to prove an impossible dream.

Kaiser would instead direct JV 44's operations from the ground at both the Feldkirchen operations centre and at Riem. While he arranged the tactical control of the jets in the air, Gutowski handled liaison with the various command staffs and organisations, as well as making sure that the ground support organisation at Riem was functioning efficiently.

During the first days of April 1945, Steinhoff persisted with at least some rudimentary training on the Me 262 for his more willing – and able – pilots. For Krupinski, hardly had he departed the comforts of 'Florida' than he found himself in the cockpit of an Me 262 for the first time;

'The next day – 2 April – I was sitting in the cockpit of an Me 262 at Riem. I had a hell of a bad head – the result of too many drinks the night before. Steinhoff was standing on the port wing. He said, "The most difficult thing with this type of aircraft is to start the engines – I'll do that for you". There was no reading any manuals or anything like that. There was no training programme. He just gave me some basic information – enough to get started.

'Actually, I found that taking off in the Me 262 was fairly easy because the nose wheel rolled nice and smoothly, but the problem was that the engines didn't accelerate fast enough. You needed the whole length of the airfield before you reached an adequate take-off speed. I prepared myself – I closed the canopy, threw a quick glance over the instrument panel – brakes off – and slowly, like a lame duck, the bird began to roll. But then the end of the runway, as I predicted, came towards me very quickly. A glance at the speed indicator told me I was moving at 200 kmh.

'Pulling gently at the stick, I got into the air. No drag, and she climbed swiftly. Landing gear up. Throttle lightly back to 8000 rpm. I climbed and the speed grew and grew – 350, 400, 500, 600 kmh – there seemed to be no end to its speed. Still I climbed – it was fantastic! I levelled out, my speed slowly approaching 900 kmh.'

It was early afternoon as Krupinski headed south towards the Bavarian Alps, and as he crossed the Tegernsee, a message came over the radio from the controller at Riem warning of P-38 Lightnings approaching from Innsbruck. He was ordered to return, but Krupinski chose to press on. As he approached the city, he quickly spotted the distinctive twin-boom shape of the American fighters – they were long-range escort fighters from the US Fifteenth Air Force.

Approaching them at 900 kmh, Krupinski lined up the first one and closed on it in the hope of claiming a P-38 on his first flight in the Me 262. A pursuit ensued over the rooftops of Innsbruck, with Krupinski opening fire with his 30 mm MK 108 cannon. But his efforts were in vain – the veteran *Jagdflieger* watched in dismay as the P-38 slid away beneath him, and as the Me 262 powered forward, too fast;

'It was just the same as in the early days against the Russians when they flew those old biplanes like the I-153 and the I-16 Ratas, and we flew the Bf 109 – there was such a difference in speed and you had to compensate, and I didn't.'

As he touched down back at Riem, Krupinski struggled to master the power of the jet and was forced to roll off the runway. Nevertheless, as he later informed Steinhoff, he realised that in the Me 262 the Luftwaffe had the machine with which to fight back against the Allies.

Meanwhile, in Berlin, Gollob was not happy with what was happening at Riem and the initial performance of Galland's dissident unit. In a report to Göring he complained that JV 44 had achieved nothing, and that it had adopted 'other operational methods which detract from those that are commonly accepted. It is proposed to disband the unit and to deploy its pilots more purposefully with other units'. This was perhaps an unfair accusation in view of the fact that the *Verband* was still training – although Krupinski's fruitless encounter with the P-38s did herald the start of simultaneous combat operations.

At 1100 hrs on 4 April, Leutnant Fährmann and Unteroffizier Schallmoser took off from Riem to engage 12 P-38s from the Fifteenth Air Force that were approaching Munich at a altitude of 10,000 metres. As the jets closed head-on with the American aircraft, Schallmoser found his four MK 108 30 mm cannon to be inoperable when he attempted to open fire. Cursing his bad luck, he momentarily looked down to his instrument panel, whereupon he realised that he had not correctly flipped away the safety guard over the firing button on his control column! It was a fateful distraction.

Looking up again, to his horror, Schallmoser realised that he was on a collision course with one of the Lightnings, and he desperately attempted to veer away – but to almost no avail. At an incredibly high closing speed,

Me 262s of JV 44 lined up on the grass at the edge of Munich-Riem in April 1945. Note the starting generator carts near the two aircraft to the left of the photograph, the nearest of which is Me 262 'White 5', Wk-Nr. 111745 – an aircraft flown by more than one of the unit's pilots

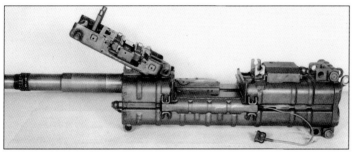

Above and left
The Rheinmetall-Borsig 30 mm MK 108 cannon, which was good for close-range fire against heavy bombers. Although a powerful weapon, its cheapness and ease of manufacture made it prone to jamming and other forms of malfunction

the Me 262 'grazed' the P-38's tail unit with the tip of its starboard wing. In seconds, Schallmoser had managed to form up with Fährmann and, somewhat shaken, he returned to Riem. As he banked away, Schallmoser caught sight of the Lightning spiralling towards the ground and its pilot bailing out.

That evening it was reported that an Me 262 of *'Jagdverband Galland'* had destroyed one enemy reconnaissance aircraft during operations over southern Germany. Although Schallmoser's jet sustained only minor damage, his collision came as a warning to the less experienced pilots of JV 44 to be very aware of the extreme speed of the Me 262.

The next day it was to be Fährmann's turn to be shaken. Just after 1030 hrs, JV 44 despatched five Me 262s to the northeast, led by Oberst Steinhoff, to intercept some of the 1000 US Eighth Air Force heavy bombers that were striking at transport targets and airfields in southern Germany. Flying with Steinhoff were Krupinski, Fährmann, Oberfeldwebel Nielinger and another, unidentified pilot. The Me 262s intercepted B-17s of the 379th BG over Straubing and accounted for one *'Viermot'* shot down, although an American post-mission report described JV 44's attack as 'unaggressive and uncoordinated'.

During the engagement, Fährmann, who was experiencing problems with one of his engines, was attacked by the fighter escort and was forced to bail out over the Danube. He parachuted into trees close to the river and was later cut down by some farm workers, who took him to a nearby farm where he was interviewed by the local mayor in an attempt to establish and confirm his identity! The mayor eventually telephoned Munich-Riem to report Fährmann's safety. The pilot was returned to Riem in a motorcycle sidecar at daybreak the following day.

A standard four-gun configuration of MK 108 30 mm cannon as installed in the nose of an Me 262A-1a. Pilots quickly discovered that the relatively slow rate-of-fire from the belt-fed, electrically-ignited MK 108 dramatically reduced the weapon's effectiveness in combat in the fast-flying Me 262

Feldwebel Josef Dobnig (second from left in the foreground) and Unteroffizier Eduard Schallmoser (with his hand on his collar) gather on the grass close to JV 44's dispersal at Riem for a discussion. Note the far end of the Riem workshops and hangars in the background

As the remaining Me 262s landed at Riem, they did so minutes after a flight of P-51s had strafed the airport. With only one of his MK 108s functioning, Steinhoff was nevertheless able to give a brief pursuit and damage one of the Mustangs as they made off.

A new, deadly addition to the Me 262's armoury was ordered the same day that Steinhoff's small formation attacked the 379th BG when instructions were issued to the Luftwaffe's armament experimental unit (Oberst Georg Christl's *Jagdgruppe* 10 at Redlin) to furnish Galland's unit with the new 55 mm R4M air-to-air rocket.

For some time, German weapons experts had realised that the installation of rockets would become increasingly necessary as an alternative to fighter aircraft being loaded with more and more fixed guns. Unguided projectiles were seen as a more effective form of firepower when tackling heavily defended American bomber formations.

Throughout the latter half of 1943 and into 1944, both German fighter and heavy fighter units operating in the defence of the Reich had been equipped with the relatively primitive, and hastily converted, tube-launched, spin-stabilised Army 21 cm *Werfer-Granate* mortar shell in an attempt to break up heavy bomber formations through blast effect. But the weapon proved generally inaccurate, and successes were negligible, with only isolated impact being made on a tightly formed bomber *Pulk*.

The R4M was intended to overcome this by being fired at ranges of up to 800 metres. It took the form of an 55 mm calibre, unrotated, rail or tube-launched, solid fuel propelled, multi-fin stabilised missile some 814 mm in length, with the warhead contained in a thin 1 mm sheet steel case enclosed in two pressed steel sections welded together and holding a Hexogen 520 g high-explosive charge. It weighed 3.5 kg.

Three views of JV 44's Me 262 'White 5' (Wk-Nr. 111745), seen parked in the unit's 'start area' at Munich-Riem. The aircraft was one of a number operated by the unit which were finished typically in a very plain application of Dunkelgrün 83 on their fuselages and uppersurfaces, with Blue-Grey 76 on their undersides. This aircraft was flown by several of JV 44's pilots

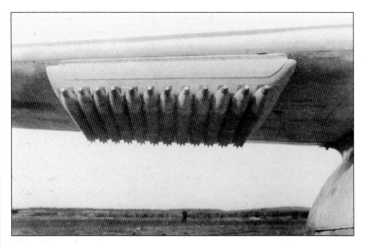

Left
This Me 262 boasts a dozen 55 mm R4M missiles fitted to a wooden launch rack outboard of its starboard Jumo 004 jet engine

Below
The 55 mm R4M air-to-air rocket in its two basic variants – the top one is the armour-piercing version as carried by the Me 262, while the bottom weapon is fitted with a high-explosive warhead

Bottom
A dismantled R4M air-to-air rocket with its tail fins extended, showing internal fittings and the explosive charge

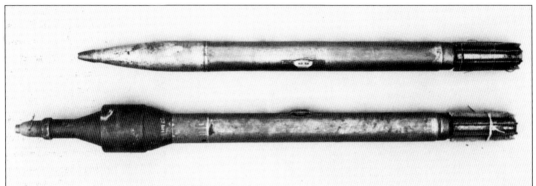

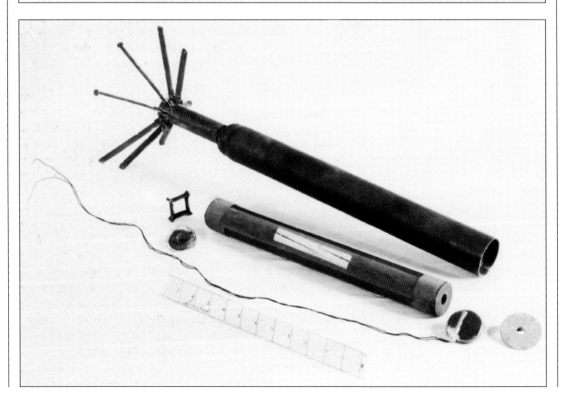

A maximum load of 12 R4Ms could be fitted to an Me 262, utilising 0.7 metre-long, 21 kg wooden under-wing racks fitted outboard of the engines, with each rocket boasting sliding lugs so that it could hang freely from the guide rails. However, as many rails as desired could be fitted together to make one launch rack with a gap of 65 mm between each rail. It was calculated that the loss of speed incurred to an Me 262 as a result of the rack being fitted was approximately 16 kmh.

Adolf Galland recounted;

'On the Me 262, we could mount the R4M outside of the turbines under the wings, 12 on each side, with little aerodynamic disturbance. They were fired via a switch relay in 0.03-second gaps, the rockets being aimed in exactly the same way as the MK 108, with a natural dispersion of about 35 square metres. But on account of the arrangement of the rockets, a shotgun-like pattern was made creating a rectangle around the bomber. One hit – any hit – no matter where it was scored, sufficed to destroy a four-engined bomber.

'The loss of speed from the Me 262 as a result of mounting the R4M was insignificant. The rocket projectiles were mounted with an upward inclination of eight degrees and fired some 600 metres from the target. At this range they had the same ballistics as MK 108 cannon shells. When you fired them, you just heard "sssshhhh" – just a whisper.'

Johannes Steinhoff recalled even greater range capability;

'The great advantage of the rockets was that although their speed only slightly exceeded that of sound, they could be let off 1100 metres away from the target – and when fired from this range they represented a field-of-fire in excess of 30 metres x 14 metres. This meant that by releasing all his rockets at once against a close formation of bombers, a pilot couldn't miss. We had, at last, the means not only of combating these hitherto almost unassailable formations, but of destroying them too. But – and it is a big "but" – it was "five minutes to twelve", in other words early April 1945, before we got the rocket armament, and then only enough to equip a few aircraft.'

Indeed, JV 44's operating strength numbered only 'a few' aircraft – on 6 April the unit reported 18 Me 262s available, of which just seven were serviceable. With such low operating numbers, combat attrition was deeply felt. On the afternoon of 8 April, Feldwebel Kammerdiener, flying on his first operational patrol in an Me 262, was bounced by American fighters near Riem and his aircraft, 'White 8', was damaged in the starboard engine, forcing him to make a single-engine landing.

The next day, conditions at Riem worsened considerably when 228 B-17s of the US Eighth Air Force, escorted by nearly 200 P-51s bombed the airport and inflicted fragmentation damage on six of JV 44's Me 262s. The control tower, administration and accommodation buildings were bombed and the main hangar and two adjoining hangars were badly damaged by incendiaries. The perimeter tracks and taxiways were also hit, an ammunition storage area was left burning and dispersals badly damaged by high explosive blasts. Six personnel were killed in the raid and another 50 wounded – including two from JV 44.

The main east-west runway was hit several times and left pitted with craters, yet Unteroffizier Müller was able to take off in the late afternoon in Me 262 'White 5' (one of JV 44's most active aircraft) to chase the

CHAPTER ONE

S.A. 3543
MUNICH/RIEM AIRFIELD
9 APR 1945

APPROXIMATE BOMB PLOT

Concentration of H.E. bursts.
Area of H.E. bursts.
Area of I.B. bursts.
Area of fragmentation bursts.
Fire.
Outline of target area.

Photographic background: 32S/406-5022
Neg. No. PP-305573

On 9 April 1945, a heavy air attack by more than 200 bombers of the US Eighth Air Force inflicted severe damage on Munich-Riem, including its main buildings and hangars. JV 44 lost two of its personnel. This American post-raid photograph illustrates the extent of the damage

home-bound bombers. Despite his superior speed, the fighter escorts managed to hold him at bay, and Müller returned safely, but without success. Galland recorded;

'The most unpleasant attacks were the ones in which they used small fragmentation bombs – they caused incredible damage to the aircraft, vehicles and equipment. However, these small bombs didn't render the airfield useless. You could land again – even with fighters – once some of the fragments had been cleared. The craters didn't even need filling up, as they were shallow.

'Attacks with heavy bombs didn't affect the aircraft on the airfield, as they caused relatively little damage even when they exploded quite near. The danger was not so much the bombs themselves as the rubble, stones, fragments and things of that sort which were thrown up by the exploding ordnance. They penetrated the aircraft. The craters made the airfield useless, and then it was a question of how much manpower and machinery we had to clear the place up. There was a definite lack of construction machinery such as tractors, dredgers and bulldozers with which to fill in the craters.'

Two more views of Me 262 'White 5' Wk-Nr. 111745 at Munich-Riem in April 1945. It was flown variously by Unteroffizier Johann-Karl Müller, Unteroffizier Eduard Schallmoser and almost certainly by other pilots too. The aircraft's Werknummer is in black and the uppersurface Dunkelgrün 83 runs to the edge of the undersides

Adolf Galland told his interrogators immediately after the war that such was the supremacy of Allied air power over Munich-Riem in April 1945 that 'American fighter-bombers would even attack a stray dog'. A hurried – and seemingly dubious – solution to this problem was the digging of 'one-man foxholes' around JV 44's dispersal area, into which both pilots and groundcrew could take refuge during an enemy air attack. Here, Unteroffizier Eduard Schallmoser (right) playfully wields a shovel over a fellow airman's head in a brief attempt to alleviate the tedium of digging such a hole

American air superiority had become a fact of life – particularly the despised *Jabos*. According to Galland, 'The saying was that the American fighter-bombers would even attack a stray dog'.

On 10 April, three Me 262s were destroyed and another three damaged during a low-level attack by P-51s of the 353rd FG. In response, the redoubtable 'Jonny' Müller scrambled again from Riem mid-morning in 'White 5' to intercept a flight of P-47s, probably from the Ninth Air Force's 36th FG, over Augsburg. Müller shot down one of the American fighters over the city and returned to Riem an hour later. But worse was to come. By the end of the day, of 13 newly delivered Me 262s, JV 44 reported 11 as destroyed by enemy action, with another lost due to 'other causes'. The *Oberkommando der Luftwaffe* (OKL) signalled;

'Available jet and rocket airfields are being neutralised by strong Allied fighter forces, thus impeding the landing of our own units after operations. Alternative landing facilities are therefore of decisive significance.'

A list was drawn up of around 70 emergency airfields throughout southern Germany and Austria from which jet units could operate. Orders were issued to ensure that these fields held adequate stocks of jet fuel. Furthermore, OKL briefly considered moving JV 44, as well as elements of III./EJG 2, to northern Italy in the event that Riem was captured by the Americans. Two airfields northeast of Milan, one near Bergamo, one west of Lake Garda and another northwest of Treviso were considered, all of which had runways of sufficient length to conduct jet operations as already proven by virtue of the fact that Ar 234 jet reconnaissance aircraft had been flying from Udine and Lonnate-Pozzolo since March. A plentiful stock of J2 jet fuel was kept at both sites too.

Had JV 44 transferred to Italy, then the unit's Jumo 004 jet engines could have been serviced at underground workshops already built on the western shore of Lake Garda. The Junkers factory in Prague had been placed on standby to deliver the necessary jigs and spare parts, and supply depots had been organised around Vicenza. In the end, however, nothing came of this idea.

Despite such hectic operating conditions, pilots of various ranks continued to arrive at Riem to report to Galland. Knight's Cross-holder, Major Werner Roell, a veteran Stuka pilot who had flown nearly 500 missions over the Balkans, the Mediterranean and Russia, had been transferred to Kammhuber's Jet Aircraft Plenipotentiary staff (see Chapter 2). Kammhuber promptly despatched Roell to Riem, where he was to assist Galland in making sure the local facilities were able to support JV 44's presence there.

Roell was followed by a stellar trio of *'Experten'* who would ensure that – if nothing else – *Jagdverband* 44 would go on to enjoy a reputation like no other in the history of the Luftwaffe. Some time in mid-April, JV 44 was boosted by the arrival of Major Gerhard Barkhorn, who had recently left command of JG 6 on or around 9-10 April, where he had flown the Fw 190D-9 in the defence of the Reich.

A recipient of the Knight's Cross with Oakleaves and Swords, Barkhorn had scored his 301st aerial victory on 14 November 1944, making him the second highest-scoring fighter pilot in the Luftwaffe. Understandably, the path to this position had been fraught with danger, and on 31 May 1944, while leading II./JG 52 in the East – and on his sixth mission of the day – he had fallen prey to a Russian fighter, during which he suffered severe wounds to his right arm and leg. Barkhorn never fully recovered, and his departure from JG 6 was a reflection of the wounds which continued to plague him. Nevertheless, following a brief period of hospitalisation at Bad Wiessee, he transferred to JV 44 and reported for operations.

Barkhorn was joined by another Knight's Cross holder, Major Wilhelm Herget. The diminutive Herget – known as *'der Kleine'* ('Tiny') to his friends – had earned a venerable reputation within the nightfighter arm. While *Kommandeur* of I./NJG 4 in June 1943, he was awarded the Knight's Cross for his 30th victory. However, his greatest accomplishment came on the night of 20 December that year, when he downed eight RAF bombers in 50 minutes. One of his victims that night was claimed using only four rounds of ammunition. In this attack, he had manoeuvred his Bf 110 below the targeted Lancaster, and using the bomber's engine exhaust as a guide, waited until he could see the reflection from the exhaust in his mirror before opening fire.

The Oakleaves were awarded to Herget by Hitler in April 1944 to mark his 63rd victory, but in January 1945 he was transferred away from operational duties and attached to the staff of the *Sonderkommission Kleinrath* – a special investigative body charged with eliminating bottle-necks in the test-flying and delivery schedules of newly manufactured aircraft. Herget became involved in developing ways of improving production of the Me 262, but in doing so he highlighted weaknesses in the slave labour system used by certain Messerschmitt

Like Walter Krupinski, Major Gerhard Barkhorn joined JV 44 from the fighter pilots' recuperation facility at Bad Wiessee. A recipient of the Knight's Cross with Oakleaves and Swords, Barkhorn was the second highest-scoring fighter pilot in the Luftwaffe, but he did not enjoy flying the Me 262. Nominally, he was placed in charge of JV 44's motor transport

Major Wilhelm Herget, who was a Knight's Cross holder and eminent nightfighter ace, was suffering from disillusion with the political leadership of the Third Reich when he joined JV 44 in April 1945. Like Galland, he too had fallen foul of Göring and been removed from operations to undertake staff work. He would play an intriguing role in the last days of JV 44's existence

sub-contractors, and subsequently fell foul of Göring, who promptly forbade him from setting foot in another factory.

Willi Herget duly returned to what he was best at, and visited the Lechfeld test centre on 5 April 1945 to carry out trials with a new and extraordinary variant of the jet fighter. The Me 262A-1a/U4 was a standard Me 262 fitted with a long-barrelled Mauser 50 mm MK 214 cannon in the nose space normally reserved for the four smaller MK 108s.

The origins of such a dubious configuration are believed to lie with Hitler, who had lent his support for the idea in January 1945 after envisaging a weapon able to bring down bombers from outside their defensive fire cone. Projecting some two metres from the nose, the MK 214 possessed a muzzle velocity of 920 metres per second. The weapon had been test-fired 128 times before malfunctioning.

Once repaired, Herget took over, and was able to fire another six shots against ground targets before attempting to use the MK 214 in anger on 16 April against American bomber formations. On both occasions, however, the gun jammed yet again. Despite this, a second machine was equipped with the MK 214, but it is unlikely that it ever saw use. Herget is then thought to have flown the first Me 262A-1a/U4 to Munich-Riem, where it was placed on charge with JV 44 – probably to the considerable consternation of the unit's pilots.

One of the leading 'mutineers', Oberst Günther Lützow, also arrived at Riem from 'exile', having recently vacated the post of regional fighter leader in northern Italy. He had apparently requested, and obtained approval, to join Galland's *Jagdverband* from none other than the man who had angrily banished him to Italy in the first place, Hermann Göring. Galland wrote;

Following trials at Lechfeld, Major Herget flew Me 262A-1a/U4 Wk-Nr. 111899 to JV 44 at Riem. The jet, fitted with an ungainly 50 mm Mauser MK 214 cannon, is believed to have been used in action on two occasions by JV 44, but with no result. One US airman who witnessed the aircraft in the air described the cannon as resembling 'a giant telephone pole'

'"Franzl" became my closest friend in those last weeks. I shall always remember him as an outstanding example of a German fighter pilot – upright, courageous and cheerful. Having overcome some initial problems, flying the Me 262 operationally became his last, great passion.'

At this point Galland refined the leadership structure of JV 44, possibly envisaging the unit to grow still further, by appointing Lützow as his Adjutant, to whom a signals officer (Hauptmann Montanus) and a combat victory record-keeper (Hauptmann Vollmer, a reserve officer who also happened to supply Galland with his favourite brand of cigars!) would report.

In addition, Steinhoff became Operations Officer, with Major Hohagen as Technical Officer (although an Allied radio decrypt of 3 April suggests JG 7 was asked to transfer Obersting. Franz Frodl to JV 44 for the same role), Oberleutnant Blomert as Navigational Officer and Major Schnell in charge of airfield infrastructure, all reporting to him. Hauptmann Kessler, formerly on the staff of the *General der Jagdflieger*, would serve as Galland's personal adjutant with reservist Hauptmann Sprotte as Maintenance Officer and Barkhorn in the somewhat unlikely role of managing the motor transport pool.

Assisting Steinhoff was Hauptmann Gutowski, who managed the Battle HQ at Feldkirchen and was in contact via a dedicated landline with Oberfeldwebel Kaiser, who maintained direct contact with the pilots from a tent close to dispersal. Kaiser had the unenviable task of having to remain at his post during Allied air attacks. Later, take-off and landing procedures were observed from the roof of a radio truck parked close to the perimeter track to the northeast of the landing ground, and not far from the unit's dispersal hut.

Oberst Günther Lützow (centre) arrived for duty with JV 44 at Riem in early April 1945, Galland immediately appointing the 108-victory *Experte* as his adjutant. He is seen here in conversation with Oberst Günther von Maltzahn (left), the *Jafü Italien* (Fighter Commander Italy) and Oberst Hannes Trautloft, commander of the 4. *Fliegerschule-division*, in the courtyard of the Feldkirchen orphanage which served as JV 44's Battle Headquarters. Both von Maltzahn and Trautloft had been directly involved alongside Lützow in making representations to Göring in late 1944 over what they perceived as poor management of the Luftwaffe at high command-level

Oberst Günther Lützow (left) and Oberst Johannes Steinhoff prepare for a daily briefing outside the wooden hut which JV 44 occupied as its dispersal at Munich-Riem. Steinhoff recorded that this area 'was a masterpiece of improvisation, consisting basically of a table and a few rickety chairs set up in the middle of a patch of weeds and undergrowth'. Note the motorcycle used as a form of transport around the airfield. Steinhoff and Lützow effectively held operational command of the *Jagdverband* during the first half of April 1945

Thus it was that by mid-April 1945, commanded by Adolf Galland and numbering among its ranks some of the most highly decorated *'Experten'* in the *Jagdwaffe*, JV 44 had become in a matter of a month one of the most unique units in the Luftwaffe because of its *raison d'être* and its officer cadre, who were without equal. In some quarters JV 44 was already being dubbed the 'Squadron of Aces', even if many of its members had proved 'politically incorrect', or had been evicted from other units because of insubordination, or were combat veterans declared unfit for frontline service due to fatigue or wounds, or fighter instructors without a job. Undeniably, it was extraordinary, and it still functioned with a degree of autonomy. Yet operating conditions were quite primitive; as Johannes Steinhoff recorded;

'The squadron's mess area was a masterpiece of improvisation, consisting basically of a table and a few rickety chairs set up in the middle of a patch of weeds and undergrowth. A field telephone stood on the table. The pilots lounged in deckchairs sipping coffee out of chunky Wehrmacht cups. Saucers of thin red jam and a stack of damp army bread covered some of the cup rings on the stained table top and provided our sustenance.'

Throughout mid-April 1945, the city of Munich and the airport at Riem were bombed and strafed again and again – by day and night. Yet, paradoxically, higher up the Luftwaffe chain of command, it seemed ignorance of reality reigned supreme. On the night of 10/11 April, the Luftwaffe *Führungsstab* began issuing preparatory orders for elements of JG 7 to vacate their airfields around Berlin – which had become almost inoperable – and transfer south to Bavaria. But *in* Bavaria, although a delivery of 12 new jets was promised for JV 44, Galland was concerned that he had nowhere safe to put them!

On 16 April, a formation of Me 262s – possibly as many as 14 – led by Galland, with some aircraft equipped with R4M rockets, took off to intercept B-26 Marauders. The *Verbandsführer* claimed two Marauders shot down and the 322nd BG is known to have lost two aircraft to enemy action. That same day, a formation of P-38s from the US Fifteenth Air Force dive-bombing a bridge on the Walchensee, 65 km south of Munich, was attacked by five Me 262s. The jets made one pass, forcing the Lightnings to jettison their bombs, and then pulled away. There were no claims and no losses on either side. It is likely that the jets were from JV 44.

Any R4Ms expended on the 16th would have been replaced by the shipment of rockets ordered to be flown to JV 44 aboard two He 111s from Lübeck-Blankensee that day.

The pilots of JV 44 assemble to receive the orders of the day from Oberst Lützow and Oberst Steinhoff at the unit's dispersal area. Identifiable, from left to right, are Major Erich Hohagen, Hauptmann Walter Krupinski, Oberst Günther Lützow (standing in leather overcoat), Oberst Johannes Steinhoff (seated centre), Leutnant Blomert (leaning against hut), Unteroffizier Eduard Schallmoser (standing in forage cap), Fahnen-junker Oberfeldwebel Klaus Neumann (seated on arm of chair in forage cap) and Oberleutnant Klaus Faber (of the *Platzschutzschwarm*, standing in officer's cap). Note the field telephone and flare pistols on the table

Oberfeldwebel Rudolf Nielinger (left) grins down at the camera from the roof of the radio truck used by JV 44 to monitor the take-offs and landings of its Me 262s at Munich-Riem. With Nielinger is Oberfeldwebel Josef Dobnig, a native of Carinthia. Both men were flying instructors with fighter training units before joining JV 44

65

Oberleutnant Hans 'Specker' Grünberg joined JV 44 sometime between 17 and 27 April 1945 from his position as *Staffelkapitän* of 1./JG 7, with whom he had flown the Me 262 over the Berlin area. He is credited with scoring 82 victories in 550 missions, including the destruction of seven Il-2s in three sorties in Russia in July 1943 whilst with 5./JG 3. He was awarded the Knight's Cross in July 1944

In the early afternoon of the 17th, Galland led a formation of seven Me 262s to engage an incoming bomber formation. The jets were directed by the Battle HQ at Feldkirchen to proceed on a northerly course towards Nuremberg. Problems plagued the operation from the start, with Oberfeldwebel Nielinger being forced to turn back in 'White 12' after 20 minutes due to an undercarriage defect.

Approaching the enemy formation of 36 B-26s, Unteroffizier Schallmoser, flying 'White 10', found that his newly installed EZ 42 gyroscopic gunsight had malfunctioned. Undeterred, he flew into the midst of the *Pulk*, only to discover that his guns were jammed. Returning for a second pass, the guns 'unjammed' themselves just in time, and Schallmoser was able to record hits on one of the P-47 Thunderbolt escorts, but not without sustaining damage to his own aircraft. Return fire from the Thunderbolt left a large hole in his canopy, though Schallmoser himself was unharmed.

Luftwaffenkommando West reported that *Jagdverband 44* had accounted for one enemy aircraft shot down, with another probable. JV 44 is also reported to have lost one machine, although the identities of pilot and aircraft are unknown. As a result of these initial problems with the EZ 42, however, most of the unit's pilots simply locked the new gunsight so that it functioned like the old fixed reflector sights they were well used to.

That same day, Oberleutnant Hans Grünberg, *Staffelkapitän* of 1./JG 7, was ordered to report to JV 44. Previously, *'Specker'* Grünberg had had a long association with 5./JG 3, having joined that *Staffel* in May 1941 and been appointed its commander in May 1944. He was a fearless, capable and 'close-range' fighter pilot who, in Russia, had shot down no fewer than seven Il-2 *Sturmoviks* in three missions, and who had bailed out on four occasions. Grünberg received the Knight's Cross on account of his 70th victory in early August 1944 while flying home defence missions. He shot down at least 11 heavy bombers, including five with the Me 262.

It seems, however, that Grünberg was still with 1./JG 7 two days after he had received his transfer order, for on 19 April he claimed a B-17 shot

Oberst Johannes Steinhoff listens to updates on the air situation by telephone link from JV 44's operations room at Feldkirchen while surrounded by several of the unit's pilots. The latter are, from left to right, Hauptmann Walter Krupinski, Major Erich Hohagen, Oberst Günther Lützow (in leather overcoat), Steinhoff (seated), Fahnen-junker Oberfeldwebel Klaus Neumann (leaning forward in forage cap), Oberleutnant Klaus Faber (*Platzschutzschwarm*), Unteroffizier Eduard Schallmoser (partially obscured in forage cap) and unidentified

down over Bohemia, but once again, in the process, he had been forced to bail out of his jet fighter. However, a pilot roster list drawn up by Hauptmann Gutowski (see Appendix 1) on 27 April shows Grünberg as being on the strength of JV 44. His movements thereafter are not clear, and to date no photographic record of him with the unit has surfaced.

In the early afternoon of 18 April, word came through from the Feldkirchen war room of large masses of enemy bombers approaching from the north and south. These comprised aircraft from the US Eighth, Ninth and Fifteenth Air Forces en route to attack railway targets and fuel dumps across southern Germany and around the Prague-Pilsen areas, the 'Mighty Eighth' alone despatching 760 heavy bombers. Overwhelmingly outnumbered, JV 44 prepared to send up six Me 262s – at least half of them carrying R4Ms – to take on the bombers.

The small formation was broken down into two three-aircraft *Ketten*, with Galland leading the first *Kette*, accompanied by Oberleutnant Stigler and Leutnant Neumann, while Steinhoff, Hauptmann Krupinski and Leutnant Fährmann formed the second. The six jets were flown by what must have been one of the most illustrious groupings of Luftwaffe pilots ever assembled to fly one mission – one Generalleutnant, four holders of the Knight's Cross and five pilots accounting for almost 550 victories.

The jets were towed out to the start area by *Kettenkrad* half-tracked motorcycles and manoeuvred into a closely-formed formation to take account of the relatively narrow – and by now bomb and debris-strewn – grass strip which JV 44 used. There was the usual whine as the Jumo 004 turbojets were started up, followed by clouds of dust, before the aircraft began to take off. According to eyewitness accounts, Galland was airborne first, with Stigler next and Neumann following.

Two of JV 44's most combat-seasoned officers take a smoking break while at readiness outside the unit's dispersal hut at Riem in April 1945. Between them, by war's end, they had been credited with the destruction of 32 four-engined bombers. To left is Fahnen-junker Oberfeldwebel Klaus Neumann, formerly of IV.(*Sturm*)/JG 3 and a recipient of the Knight's Cross with 37 victories (most scored in the defence of the Reich, with 19 of them being four-engined bombers) in 200 missions. To the right is fellow Knight's Cross holder Major Erich Hohagen, who had served with JG 51, JG 2, JG 27 and JG 7 prior to joining JV 44. He is credited with 55 victories claimed over 500 missions, including 13 four-engined bombers. Note yet more of the familiar white wooden deckchairs which had apparently been commandeered by the unit!

JV 44 used semi-tracked NSU *Kettenkrad* motorcycles to move its Me 262s around the field at Riem in order to economise on J2 jet fuel. Here, Unteroffizier Eduard Schallmoser (left) sits on a *Kettenkrad* while four unidentified pilots study a document

Another view of Unteroffizier Schallmoser and three unidentified pilots of JV 44 in discussion around a *Kettenkrad* semi-tracked motorcycle tow vehicle at Munich-Riem. The airmen all wear the typical flying garb used by the unit, consisting of late-war leather flight jackets with fur-lined collars, forage caps and goggles

Behind came Steinhoff, followed by Krupinski to his left and Fährmann on the right. As the second *Kette* rolled along the strip, reaching 200 kmh, Steinhoff's port wing suddenly dropped as his mainwheel struck some debris left on the field from the previous day's bombing attack. The Me 262 began to swerve to the left, dangerously close to Krupinski, who was still powering behind. Krupinski hauled his control column back and lifted into the air just in time to avoid a collision, flying right over Steinhoff's Me 262 which was now heading irreversibly – and still at speed – towards an embankment at the end of the strip. A second or so later, Krupinski became aware of an explosion which buffeted his aircraft.

Neumann was also airborne, but realising something was very wrong, for an instant looked back – horrified – towards the ground. Steinhoff's aircraft was now an inferno. In his post-war memoirs, he wrote;

'Catapulted high into the air, the stricken bird dragged itself through several more seconds of existence. Shortly before the impact, my hands flew instinctively to the shoulder belts. I tugged so violently on the straps that my body slammed back against the seat. Then, all of a sudden, everything seemed to grow still. There was only the hissing of the huge flames. As if in slow motion, I saw a wheel go soaring through the air. Metal fragments and bits of undercarriage flew after it, spinning very slowly. Wherever I looked was red, deep red. Grasping the sides of the cockpit, I pulled myself up until I was standing on the parachute. I had got my feet over the cockpit rim when the rockets started exploding under the wings. They skittered over the field and went off with a hellish bang.

'Taking great leaping strides, I ran out along the wing to escape from the flames. And when I emerged from the inferno, and my straining lungs filled with fresh air, I sank to my knees as if under the impact of a mighty blow. I managed to get to my feet, and as I stumbled a few steps farther everything went black – my eyes had swollen shut. I became aware of piercing pain in my wrists where the flames shooting through the cockpit floor had burned off the skin between my gloves and the sleeves of my leather jacket.'

Flying through the drifting smoke, the five remaining jets continued with the mission, but it proved a fruitless sortie. When the pilots returned they were ready for the worst, certain Steinhoff had been killed. But he had escaped, saved by the self-contained metal rear cockpit sub-assembly which held the Me 262's instrument panel and electrical controls, stick and rudder, throttles, seat and battery, and which was intended to break free on impact.

Smoke rises out of the charred remains of Oberst Johannes Steinhoff's Me 262 following its crash whilst taking off from Riem on 18 April 1945 after the aircraft had hit debris on the runway. Miraculously, Steinhoff, a veteran of some 900 combat missions, survived, although he suffered severe burns

The extent of the crash can be seen from this photograph, showing one of the Jumo 004 engine units from Steinhoff's aircraft lying some way away from the main wreckage. Note the cowling panels to the right with the ports for the MK 108 cannon clearly visible

Steinhoff was taken to the military hospital at Oberföhring. His war was over, and he would remain visibly scarred from the events of 18 April 1945 for the rest of his life.

Also on the 18th, JV 44 was reinforced by the arrival at Munich-Riem of the Me 262s of 4./KG(J) 54, the *Staffel* having been ordered to hand all its remaining jets over to Galland before transferring its entire personnel to the 'aircraftless' II./KG(J) 54. At the same time, the dissolution of this famous *Kampfgeschwader* continued with the entire III./KG(J) 54 also receiving orders to hand over its aircraft to JV 44, and thereupon cease functioning as an operational unit. An advanced detachment of Me 262s allocated to JV 44 from this unit left Neuburg the same day and headed for the transit field at Erding where, having landed, they were almost immediately subjected to an attack by American B-26s, which resulted in nearly all the aircraft being destroyed.

Pilots of 7./KG(J) 54 in discussion on the flightline at Neuberg an der Donau in March 1945. On 18 April 1945, the 4. *Staffel* of this bomber *Geschwader*, which had been converted to jet fighter operations on the initiative of IX. *Fliegerkorps*, was ordered to hand its Me 262s over to JV 44, and shortly thereafter, similar orders were issued to III./KG(J) 54. The Me 262 in this photograph carries one of several unusual finishes which were applied to aircraft of this unit

Meanwhile, Steinhoff's incapacitation forced a restructuring of JV 44, with Major Hohagen taking over as Operations Officer and Oberleutnant Stigler becoming Technical Officer. Yet more senior officers such as Lützow and Barkhorn were still grappling with the flight characteristics of the jet fighter. Barkhorn, for example, almost decapitated himself while making an emergency landing near Riem under pursuit by a P-51 when the already open canopy of his Me 262, which was suffering from a failed engine, fell closed as it hit the ground, striking the pilot on his neck. He survived, but, like Steinhoff, was admitted to hospital.

On 19 April JV 44 despatched three Me 262s to intercept B-26 Marauders (probably from the 322nd BG) that had just bombed the railway bridge at Donauwörth. Attacking from the rear of the bombers, the Germans claimed one Marauder shot down, but they actually damaged two. The Americans claimed that they had been attacked by eight to ten jets!

By early mid-April, unit commanders and intelligence officers in the US Ninth and Fifteenth Air Forces were becoming increasingly worried about the impact the German jets were having on their bomber crews. Generally speaking, it seems that intelligence on the Me 262 – and subsequent onward advice to the crews – had, for one reason or another, not been as forthcoming as perhaps it could have been.

How fast, and to what degree, information on how to deal with the jet threat had passed from the Eighth Air Force, which had had to deal with the German jets in the north, to the tactical medium bomber units of the Ninth is not known. However, the recollections of B-26 Marauder crews involved in operations at this time indicate that they were not entirely prepared for the shock encounters they had with high-speed, jet-powered interceptors firing 30 mm cannon and 55 mm rockets.

JV 44's tactics for attacking enemy bombers were greatly influenced by the low number of machines and pilots available for operations at any one time. It was quite usual for the *Jagdverband* to have just six serviceable jets available for operations, and wherever possible, with such numbers, Galland and Steinhoff tended to favour the deployment of their Me 262s in *Ketten* (the tried and tested element of three aircraft), as opposed to the more commonly used four aircraft formation – the *Schwarm* – as adopted by piston-engined fighter units. The *Kette* was also preferred by JV 44 since, on most runways, it allowed three aircraft to take off, side-by-side.

Once airborne, the aircraft in a *Kette* would be staggered below and/or behind each other, but rarely behind and above since the unsatisfactory field of vision from the Me 262 precluded this. Respective *Ketten* would fly at 300-metre intervals.

As a result of the Me 262's lack of manoeuvrability, formations in elements larger than *Ketten* were more difficult. Once visual contact was made with a bomber formation, one group was selected as the target and the jets would manoeuvre behind it so as to mount their attack from the rear. Getting into an effective attack position, however, at a range of about 1000 metres on a dead-level approach was often challenging due to the great speed and turning radius of the Me 262. Decisions regarding the attack had to be made quickly, therefore, and often at great distances from the target. This in turn made it difficult for formation leaders to correctly assess the bombers' range, course and altitude.

Furthermore, the very speed of the Me 262 – its greatest tactical advantage – curtailed the time available to a pilot when it came to scoring hits on a target. Galland recalled;

'My pilots were authorised to open fire from 600 metres. They were also permitted to fire a short burst before that if they noticed that they were being fired upon by the bombers. We also fired our rockets at that range. We often hit two bombers with them in one go.

'The Me 262 could only count on success in attacking formations of heavy bombers if they were able to approach in fairly close formation, and not if they approached at great distances apart. The *Kette* had to at least remain at one height, a clear-cut allocation of targets had to be made and the whole *Kette* had to fire simultaneously in order to disperse the defensive fire of the bombers.

'From 600 metres onwards, you had to fly in a perfectly straight line whilst starting your offensive fire. You had to break off your attack once you got to within 150 metres of the bomber, making sure to always break away above your target. On no account could you afford to turn away from the bomber while still directly behind it, thus exposing your belly to its defensive fire – you would almost certainly have been hit. But, if you had approached to within 150 metres, there was only one way out, and that was to turn away as close as possible, passing over the whole bomber formation. In any case, it was dangerous to turn away by flying underneath, as pieces of shot-down bombers, men bailing out, jettisoned bombs or burning aircraft flew straight into your face, or into your turbines.'

On 20 April, as Adolf Hitler celebrated his birthday under a rain of American bombs in Berlin, JV 44 put up a formation of Me 262s during the late morning against B-26 Marauders of the 323rd BG, which was targeting the marshalling yards at Memmingen. Just after 1100 hrs, and under clear blue skies, the Me 262s (at least some of which were carrying R4M rockets) climbed to attack the tightly-packed bombers from the east in loosely formated *Ketten* at 3000-4000 metres over the Kempten-Memmingen area.

On this occasion, the R4Ms were to prove deadly. A burst of fire from an Me 262's 30 mm cannon had shattered the port engine of B-26 *Can't Get Started* of the 454th BS, piloted by 1Lt Dale E Sanders, and it was already trailing black smoke when a 55 mm rocket speared into its fuselage. TSgt Robert M Radlein, a gunner in a neighbouring bomber, watched in horror as the Me 262s came in to attack. Then, looking out of his window, he saw Sanders' aircraft career across the sky. He recalled;

'Our top turret gunner, SSgt Edmundo Estrada, started firing. He had raised his guns straight up and was shooting at an Me 262 passing overhead. He yelled, "I got him! I got him!", because he had seen all kinds of metal and debris come flying past our aeroplane. Estrada was convinced he had hit the jet, but unfortunately the pieces of metal he had seen had come not from the German fighter but from our No 3 aircraft, piloted by 1Lt Sanders.

'I looked out of my left waist window at Sanders' aeroplane as it started to drop away from the main formation, and I was able to see the entire radio compartment. The fighter attack had stripped away all the metal from the top of the wing, as well as the compartment for the radio man and navigator – I guess from just aft of the windows in the pilot's compartment. And, of course, one engine was also gone. As I watched the bomber falling out of formation, I reached over to snap on my chest pack parachute – things were warming up pretty fast.'

Flying in 'White 11', Unteroffizier Schallmoser was one of the first pilots from JV 44 to attempt to open fire on the B-26s, but his MK 108 cannon jammed. Once again – as he had done on 4 April – Schallmoser quickly looked down at his gun firing button, and as he did so, the Me 262 took him dangerously close to the bomber formation. When Schallmoser looked up, it was too late.

Attracting fire from the Marauder gunners, 'White 11' scraped into the starboard engine propeller blades of the B-26 piloted by Lt James M. Hansen of the 455th BS. Upon impact, the jet rolled over and nosed down through the enemy formation streaming black smoke, with pieces of its own debris falling behind it. One American gunner reported seeing 'parts of the right wing break away'.

Hansen, however, was able to control his aircraft – even keeping the right-hand engine running, despite the blades having been evenly bent six inches from their tips – and returned successfully to base.

Good fortune would remain with Schallmoser, for having successfully bailed out of his plummeting aircraft, he parachuted into his mother's garden in the small town of Lenzfried-im-Allgau! Folding up his parachute and suffering from a painful blow to one of his knees as he left his aircraft, he limped into his family home, where his bewildered mother fed him with a plate of pancakes. Shortly after however, Schallmoser

Curious American groundcrew inspect the propeller blades of 1Lt James M Hansen's B-26 Marauder of the 323rd BG upon its successful return to Denain-Prouvy, in France, following its collision with Unteroffizier Eduard Schallmoser's Me 262 over Memmingen on 20 April 1945

Unteroffizier Eduard Schallmoser poses for a family snapshot with his mother in the garden of the family home near Munich on 20 April 1945. He had just bailed out of his Me 262, having collided with a B-26 of the 323rd BG piloted by 1Lt James M Hansen

joined Steinhoff in the military hospital, where he would remain until 25 April undergoing treatment to his injured knee.

Meanwhile, Unteroffizier Müller had also attacked the bombers in his 'White 15'. His R4M rockets streaked towards the bombers and two were hit. One rocket fired by JV 44 hit *Ugly Duckling*, the aircraft of 1Lt James L Vining of the 455th BS, who recalled;

'In a fast glance over my shoulder, I saw a jet rapidly approaching us in a slight turn, with muzzle flashes around the four 30 mm cannon in the nose. I turned my attention back to my position, tucking my wing closer to No 4, and at that instant a terrific blast went off below my knees and the aeroplane rolled to the right.

'Sensing that my right leg was gone, I looked toward my co-pilot, and while ordering him to take his controls, I noted that the right engine was at idle speed. So, in one swift arcing motion with my right hand, I hit the feathering button, moved to the overhead rudder trim crank and trimmed the aeroplane for single engine operation and – just as rapidly – pressed the intercom button to order the bombardier to jettison the two tons of bombs. We were losing altitude at 2000 ft per minute, which slowed to 1000 ft per minute with the load gone.'

As Vining's B-26 fell away from its formation, the relatively inexperienced co-pilot took control of the aircraft while the radio operator/navigator applied a tourniquet to Vining's shattered leg, together with some morphine. As a lone 'straggler', *Ugly Duckling* began to attract more attacks from the German jets, which attempted to finish the stricken bomber off. Miraculously, despite the substantial damage inflicted by the R4M, and a later attack by more Me 262s from I./KG(J) 54, the Marauder remained airborne and managed to return to Allied-held territory. It eventually crash-landed on an abandoned airfield in Bavaria, the bomber breaking its back in a tank-trap ditch.

By the time JV 44's Me 262s had turned away from the 323rd BG, they had shot down three B-26s and damaged a further seven. No German pilots were reported lost, but Schallmoser's aircraft was destroyed, and it is likely several others were damaged during the attack.

The next day – 21 April – both the Luftwaffe's high command infrastructure, as well as its jet fighter force, began to disintegrate. What remained of German occupied territory was split into two. Under Hitler's orders, Admiral Dönitz took over military command in the north, while Göring, who left Berlin for the last time this day, headed south. He had left General Koller in charge of the Luftwaffe, and the latter described the situation as 'catastrophic'.

Furthermore, SS-*Obergruppenführer und General der Waffen-SS Dr.Ing.* Hans Kammler, Hitler's 'Plenipotentiary for Jet Aircraft Production and Operational Deployment', signalled Göring to warn him that it was now

The shattered remains of B-26 Marauder *Ugly Duckling* of the 323rd BG lie in a tank-trap ditch in Bavaria following an attack by JV 44 using R4M rockets against the Group's formation as it targeted Memmingen on 20 April 1945. It is possible that this was one of two bombers shot down by Unteroffizier Johann-Karl Müller

impossible for the Me 262-equipped *Stab*, I. and III./JG 7 and I./KG(J) 54 to remain in the Prague area – one of the last free bastions of operations – due to there being enough fuel for only 'one operation'. And since timely supply by rail could not be guaranteed and delivery by road tanker was no longer possible, the fuel that remained would, in any case, be needed for a transfer.

Against such a doom-laden backdrop, Galland decided to address his pilots at JV 44's Feldkirchen headquarters. In blunt terms, the former *General der Jagdflieger* told his men that although, in his view, the war was over militarily, he was prepared to continue flying operations using only volunteers. He also gave them a personal assurance that whatever they chose to do, none of them would be press-ganged into joining the fighting on the ground. Galland also advised the small group of female auxiliaries who crewed the heavy flak guns on one side of the airfield that they were free to leave, and he replaced them with regular troops. But for the pilots, as Klaus Neumann recalled, 'We stayed together and we flew. We had nothing else to do. We couldn't win the war – we did it just to prove that the Me 262 was a fighter'.

This was the atmosphere into which Major Heinz Bär arrived at München-Riem, together with a small group of instructor pilots from his staff at III./EJG 2 and his long-time wingman in JG 1, Fahnen-junker Oberfeldwebel Leo Schuhmacher. With US troops just a few kilometres from III./EJG 2's base at Lechfeld, Bär took the decision to evacuate, and in the process save a small number of the jet training unit's precious aircraft, including a specially rigged Me 262 prototype variant carrying six MK 108 cannon in an adapted nose. On or around 23 April, Bär reported to Galland for duty with JV 44. His arrival was timely, for with Steinhoff in hospital, he would prove the ideal replacement, while his jet-experienced instructor pilots would serve to stiffen JV 44's ranks further.

Leo Schuhmacher had scored his first victory over Norway while flying with 2./ZG 76, before serving as a fighter instructor. He transferred to II./JG 1 in the winter of 1943, and would go on to fly some 250 missions by war's end, scoring 23 victories, of which ten were four-engined bombers. Schuhmacher had been decorated with the Knight's Cross the month before he joined JV 44.

Also among those accompanying Bär was Oberleutnant Erich Hondt, who was another experienced Reich defence pilot and former *Staffelkapitän* with I./ JG 11 who had bailed out and been wounded at least once. Hondt had left his studies in art to join the Luftwaffe at the age of 18, initially being assigned to the *Jagdgruppe Drontheim* in Norway and then JG 53 in North Africa, before joining I./JG 1 in early 1943. Wounded in June of that year following combat with American bombers, Hondt had been forced to bail out of his burning Bf 109G.

In July 1943 he was appointed commander of the *Jasta Helgoland*, with whom he flew the thoroughly obsolete Bf 109T, before leading 2./JG 11 from August to October 1943. Hondt's time in command was temporarily halted when he was badly wounded in action and forced to take to his parachute during combat with B-17s over Holland. He eventually returned to the *Staffel* in early July 1944, but was wounded again in combat in late August when set upon by P-51s over France. Hondt commanded 3./JG 11 from 15 October 1944 until March 1945,

From October 1944, Oberleutnant Erich Hondt was *Staffelkapitän* of 3./JG 11 engaged in Reich defence operations, before transferring to III./EJG 2 for jet fighter conversion in March 1945. After only a few weeks he accompanied Oberstleutnant Heinz Bär to JV 44

when he was posted to III./EJG 2, with whom he underwent training on the Me 262.

23 April 1945 also saw Major Heinrich Brücker, nominally in charge of I./KG 51's Me 262s, depart Memmingen with the *Gruppe* and head for Riem, where he too reported for duty with JV 44. 'Hein' Brücker had flown Stukas over the Balkans and Crete with III./StG 2, seeing action against the British Mediterranean Fleet. Indeed, his *Gruppe* had sunk several Royal Navy warships and thousands of tons of merchant tonnage. Brücker subsequently flew the Fw 190 in hit-and-run raids against southern England, before spending a further year as *Kommodore* of SG 4 in Italy. He was eventually posted to I./KG 51 by the *General der Schlachtflieger* in order to evaluate the Me 262 as a ground-attack aircraft. Brücker had been awarded the Knight's Cross in June 1941 following the completion of 100 combat missions.

By the evening of 23 April, JV 44 had 12 Me 262s on strength, and these were probably supplemented by the 13 jets from I./KG 51. The *Verband* was now placed under *Luftflotte* 6's Order of Battle.

With outrageous arrogance and not a little irony, Galland found himself ordered to report to a 'deeply depressed' Hermann Göring, who had recently arrived from the smoke and ruins of Berlin at his new quarters in the clear mountain air of the Obersalzberg. Galland remembered the meeting as being cordial, with the *Reichsmarschall* 'requesting details about my unit's progress in reaching operational status, officially allocating (Günther) Lützow (*Jafü Oberitalien*) to me, and reluctantly agreeing that my premonitions regarding the employment of the Me 262 crewed by bomber pilots as fighters had been right. All this was somewhat incomprehensible to me and, in reality, what he meant to

Sitting in their unit's ubiquitous white deckchairs and facing into the spring sunshine, three senior officers of JV 44 confer. They are, from left to right, newly-arrived Major Heinrich Brücker, Oberstleutnant Heinz Bär and Major Erich Hohagen. Of these three Knight's Cross holders, Brücker was unique in having served as a Stuka, ground-attack and bomber pilot. Immediately prior to joining JV 44, he had been tasked with evaluating the Me 262 as a ground-attack aircraft. Sat behind Bär, from left to right, are Oberfeldwebel Siegfried Schwaneberg (partially obscured), Fahnen-junker Oberfeldwebel Leo Schuhmacher and Oberleutnant Franz Stigler

A relieved Oberfeldwebel Leopold Knier back safely at Riem and clutching his parachute, having bailed out of a defective Me 262 over Bavaria in late April 1945

Oberfeldwebel Knier reports to Oberstleutnant Bär upon his return from bailing out of his Me 262. It seems something has been said to cause the pilots behind to smile, perhaps at Knier's expense! They are, from left to right, 'Sigi' Schwaneberg, unknown (standing), Schuhmacher, Bär, Hohagen, unknown (with eyepatch), Knier and, at far right, Kaiser

say was "Galland, you were right all along during our violent disagreements over the past few months'".

Galland bid farewell to Göring for the last time, and as they shook hands, he patted his generous stomach and admitted, 'I envy you Galland for going into action. I wish I were a few years younger and less bulky. If I were, I would gladly put myself under your command. It would be marvellous to have nothing to worry about but a good fight, like it was in the old days'.

There followed a web of intrigue, prompted by Göring's departure from the capital, which the *Führer* had viewed angrily as premature. Furthermore, in the eventuality that due to the Soviet and Allied thrusts now closing in on Berlin, Hitler was rendered incapable of continued leadership, Göring had issued his declaration of intent to assume control of Germany under terms laid down by the *Führer* in June 1941. At this, a furious Martin Bormann, Hitler's loyal private and Nazi Party Secretary, issued orders for Göring to be arrested immediately for treachery.

Hearing of this, Albert Speer, Hitler's Armaments Minister, during a final visit to the *Führer* in the Berlin bunker, managed to contact Oberst Werner Baumbach, *Kommodore* of KG 200 (the Luftwaffe's special operations wing), and request that he in turn talk with Adolf Galland at Munich-Riem. He told him to tell Galland to prevent any aircraft or facilities being made available to Göring – who was located near to the airfield at the Obersalzberg – should he attempt to escape.

How satisfied Speer was with Baumbach's response can perhaps be gauged from a subsequent letter he drafted to Galland from the *'Führer Hauptquartier'* on 23 April;

'I ask you and your comrades to do everything as discussed to prevent Göring from flying anywhere. Heil Hitler!'

Standing in the group at the rear left of this photograph, Oberfeldwebel Leopold Knier appears to be relating the events of his recent bail-out to his fellow pilots, They are, from left to right, Unteroffizier Eduard Schallmoser, Oberfeldwebel Josef Dobnig, Feldwebel Franz Steiner and Oberfeldwebel Leopold Knier. Sitting in the foreground, from left to right, are Hauptmann Walter Krupinski, Major Heinrich Brücker, Oberstleutnant Bär and Major Erich Hohagen. Sitting at rear are Oberfeldwebel Siegfried Schwaneberg (behind Bär), Fahnen-junker Oberfeldwebel Leo Schuhmacher and Oberleutnant Franz Stigler (in sunglasses)

Speer's letter never reached Galland, but several urgent telephone calls were received at Feldkirchen on the subject from various senior staff officers attached to KG 200. 'I got the impression that they had been reading too many spy stories!' Galland recalled. 'I got an order to go to Berlin to see Baumbach and Speer and to get ready to arrest Göring, but I didn't follow the order. I wanted to stay with my unit. I didn't see any reason to do what Speer proposed. I didn't see any point'.

It is ironic, but testimony to the prevailing operating conditions, that although it seems that telephone linkage to Berlin from Riem was maintained, contact between JV 44 and the neighbouring 7. *Jagddivision* had been lost when the local fighter command pulled back south towards the mountains.

Another view of the pilots of JV 44 at their dispersal at Munich-Riem in late April 1945, with visible to far right Knight's Cross holder Oberfeldwebel Herbert Kaiser – a fighter pilot who had seen combat in every war theatre, and was accredited with 68 victories. The identity of the civilian figure near the door to the dispersal hut is not known

A previously unpublished photograph of an unidentified pilot of JV 44, who can be seen laughing, fourth from left, in the group shot on page 81. He wears the typical late-war leather flight jacket worn by many members of the unit. This shot was probably taken at the same time as the group photograph – note the windows of the dispersal hut behind him

Galland wisely chose to ignore the intrigues of Berlin and got on with the job of defending the airspace over Bavaria.

24 April saw large-scale operations mounted against targets across southern Germany by the US tactical air forces. At 0950 hrs, JV 44 sent up a formation of 11 jets carrying batteries of R4M rockets and led by Oberst Lützow to engage B-26s of the 17th BG en route to bomb Schwabmünchen, to the south of Augsburg.

Twelve minutes later, the leading *Kette* of Me 262s swept towards the three Marauders forming the 'window flight' from above and behind just as it was turning away from the target area. A wave of R4Ms rippled into the small formation. It was the first time the crews of the 17th had experienced a jet attack, as Sgt Warren E Young, a gunner aboard a B-26 of the 4th BS, remembered;

'On 24 April we were attacked by jets for the first time. When I first saw an Me 262, he was coming straight for us from "five o'clock high". I opened fire, and in a matter of seconds he was overhead. I pushed the red high-speed button on my turret to turn it so that I could fire on him again as he was flying away, but before the turret had completed its 180-degree

turn, the jet had gone. As I looked over the side of our aeroplane, I saw a wing break off one of our bombers and then it went into a spin.'

One rocket had hit B-26 *STUD DUCK* of the 34th BS, piloted by 1Lt Fred J Harms. The bomber's tailplane was blasted away, and there was also damage to the wing, one of the waist gun positions and the aft section of the bomb-bay. One of *STUD DUCK's* gunners, SSgt Edward F Truver, was blown out of the aircraft, but fortunately he was wearing his parachute. The Marauder fell over to the right, narrowly avoiding collision with a neighbouring aircraft, and began to spin to earth with its gear down and bomb-bay doors blown open. It crashed into countryside

Pilots of JV 44 enjoy a joke as they sit at readiness outside their unit's dispersal hut at Munich-Riem in April 1945. Identifiable are (third from left) Feldwebel Franz Steiner, (fifth from left) Oberfeldwebel Leopold Knier, (sixth from left) Fahnen-junker Oberfeldwebel Leo Schuhmacher and (to right) Leutnant Blomert

Fighter pilots again! Generalleutnant Adolf Galland (right), with customary cigar clenched between his teeth, and Oberst Günther Lützow at readiness – *Jagdverband* 44, Munich-Riem, April 1945

Above and right
B-26 Marauder *STUD DUCK* of the
17th BG was a victim of JV 44's R4M
attack, led by Oberst Günther
Lützow, on 24 April 1945 during a
USAAF raid on Schwabmünchen.
The impact of the R4M which struck
STUD DUCK was sufficient to blow
one of its gunners out of the bomber

near the town of Babenhausen. Truver came down near the wreckage, and was the only survivor. Another R4M also claimed 34th BS B-26B *Skipper*, flown by 1Lt Leigh Slates.

Among several claims for this mission, Feldwebel Kammerdiener, flying 'White 3', was credited with one bomber confirmed shot down. JV 44 also reported the loss of an unidentified Oberfähnrich.

There was to be no let up in the action that afternoon, with the USAAF striking at a range of airfields, transport targets and oil storage and supply depots north of Munich. A force of 256 medium bombers was sent out, including 74 B-26s of the 322nd and 344th BGs, detailed to strike at an oil depot hidden in woods near Schrobenhausen, 50 km northwest of Munich, This facility was supplying fuel to German forces heading into

Accompanied by his friend and commander Adolf Galland, this is believed to be the last known photograph of Günther Lützow, taken at Munich-Riem, before his fateful mission on 24 April 1945

the so-called Alpine 'Redoubt' area, from where it was intended they would launch a desperate last stand against the approaching Allies.

A force of six Me 262s, once again led by Lützow, and including Hauptmann Krupinski and Oberleutnant Neumann, took off to the northwest to intercept. Two jets were forced to abort early due to engine or mechanical problems, but the remaining four – of which at least Lützow's and Neumann's aircraft were carrying R4Ms – swept across the Jura mountains to take on the bombers. Just before 1530 hrs, as the last element of bombers from the 344th BG was setting up to make its bomb run, the jets broke through the clouds and attacked the Marauders' window flight from high and low southeast of Monheim at a height of 7000 metres, diving to just under 3500 metres.

Sgt Jonny Quong was a top turret gunner aboard a B-26 of the 344th BG that day;

'I saw what seemed at first to be a B-26 straggler at long distance approaching us at "six o'clock". As it kept approaching, all the gunners saw it. It kept coming and then dived and broke off to the left. When it turned, I could tell it was not a B-26, but a smaller aeroplane going like a bat out of Hell. All the gunners started talking excitedly. "What the Hell was that?" We were so excited that our pilot had to tell us to keep quiet.'

Klaus Neumann immediately fired his rockets and thought he observed two Marauders break out of formation, while Krupinski saw another B-26 trailing black smoke, but managing to remain with the group.

Then, almost as fast as the jets had come, they were gone, arcing in a wide turn to port below the bombers and heading towards the cloud base in a loose formation. At that moment it seems that the P-47 Thunderbolts of the 365th FG, assigned as escorts for the Marauders, fell past the bombers in pursuit of the enemy jets. 2Lt James L Stalter, flying B-26 *Lak-a-Nookie* of the 344th BG, remembered;

'We were heading for home when I heard our Group Leader call the leader of our P-47 escort, stating "We have visitors". The fighter leader's response still sticks in my mind. In a very, very slow southern Texas drawl, he responded, "Okay, we'll be right down".'

Flying a P-47 that day was 1Lt Oliver T Cowan, leading Green Flight, who spotted the Me 262s climbing up to attack the 365th FG's charges. He flipped his big fighter over and rolled it into a sharp dive, just fast enough to catch the jets as they swept through the bombers seconds after firing their rockets;

'I recall thinking that my dive needed more speed, and I became more aware of this as the damaged jet pulled away. At this point, I suddenly realised that I was really talking out loud to my aeroplane to give more speed, and then I wondered how much of this was on the radio. We had no fear of the German jets because we could easily out-turn them. I am sure they had no fear of us either, because usually they could leave us at will. Hence, we needed altitude for speed (diving) and the element of surprise. But with the jet's speed, they could hit fast and move on.'

Leading the 365th's Blue Flight was Capt Jerry G Mast, who pushed his Thunderbolt into a full power dive in an attempt to force an Me 262 away from the bombers. He was successful. Mast's wingman, 2Lt Byron Smith Jnr, had followed his leader in his dive on the Me 262, but seconds later he had noticed another jet approaching the bombers from head-on.

Turning away from Mast, Smith closed in on the jet as it banked to the left in front of the Marauders and then executed a steep right climbing

Flying a P-47D of the 365th FG on 24 April 1945, Capt Jerry G Mast forced a Me 262 to break away from the main JV 44 attack by entering a full power dive. This was the jet that 2Lt William H Myers also pursued

turn that took it into the bomber formation. Smith levelled out at 30 degrees and fired a burst over the German machine's nose. For a moment, the Me 262 pilot continued his attack run and then must have become aware of the American fighter, for he immediately embarked upon a series of violent evasive turns and climbs. Despite this attempt to shake him off, Smith persisted in his chase and managed to fire several more bursts at the jet, which suddenly dived into the clouds. Smith at least had the satisfaction of watching his tracer strike home before being forced to return to his position and continue with the escort.

Meanwhile, Mast and 2Lt William H Myers noticed that the Me 262 they were jointly pursuing had started to pull out from its dive, but the fighter then suddenly went into an even steeper dive, its pilot having probably become aware of them following him. The jet 'went into the ground and exploded', and Myers was forced to black himself out with a high 'G' recovery in order to avoid hitting the ground himself.

For JV 44 this was a critical moment in its brief history. The jet chased by Mast and Myers was flying furthest to the south of the German group. This was Lützow's aircraft. Radio contact had apparently been lost between Lützow and the other jets, and he was observed by Krupinski to turn quite suddenly and inexplicably towards the south. Moments later, as Lützow flew away alone from the formation towards the mountains, Krupinski witnessed 'an explosion in the air';

'We broke away in a wide left turn on our homeward route. Lützow's change in course towards the south was completely incomprehensible to me, and I therefore called him on the radio, but did not get a reply. The explosion which I saw, or something very similar, occurred at a distance of at least 20 kilometres. Everyone knows that at that distance, details cannot be observed. In any case, my attempt at radio contact, prompted by Lützow's change in course, took place before I saw the explosion. We couldn't fly after him as contact with the enemy Marauders had taken place quite late into the mission, and we were compelled to fly home by the quickest route due to lack of fuel.'

The three remaining Me 262s landed back at Riem, and their pilots reported three 'probable' claims over B-26s, although the Americans reported no aircraft missing. Günther Lützow did not return, and it is

2Lt William H Myers (left) of the 388th FS/365th FG looks down from the wing of a P-47D Thunderbolt. On 24 April 1945, he chased a lone Me 262 in a steep dive and watched it hit the ground and explode. The jet is believed to have been the aircraft flown by Günther Lützow

85

believed that his Me 262 had crashed into some wasteground in the ancient town of Donauwörth, between Ulm and Ingolstadt. It was the only aircraft of this type reported as lost by the Luftwaffe that day. When Krupinski walked into the Feldkirchen operations room after the mission, he discovered that the radar signal depicting Lützow's aircraft had flashed out at roughly the same location in which he had seen the explosion.

After the war, Johannes Steinhoff commented;

'Lützow was not very familiar with the Me 262. I happened to check him out, and from the beginning I had the feeling that he was nervous somehow. He had not been in combat for a long time – more than two years. Lützow was not exactly in love with the Me 262. Did he make a mistake perhaps?'

For the pilots and groundcrew of JV 44, the loss of Günther Lützow was a severe blow. He was a decent, principled man with considerable combat experience, a fair-minded, yet focused, commander who offered inspiration to those under his command. The personality of the man and the circumstances of his death were reminiscent of the death of Manfred von Richthofen (the famous 'Red Baron') over the Western Front in April 1918. But as it was with von Richthofen's JG 1, so it was to be with Galland's JV 44 – the war went on.

The following afternoon, the unit prepared 13 Me 262s in two formations – one to carry out free-ranging patrols against enemy fighters, and the other to take on B-26 Marauders heading to Erding airfield and a neighbouring ammunition dump. Problems plagued both operations early on. Five aircraft were forced to return after take-off due to technical problems, while two more were recalled for unspecified reasons. Of those machines which continued, three encountered P-47s over Augsburg in an

While Leutnant Blomert (officer in charge of JV 44's Si 204 liaison and training aircraft) offers a light to Fahnen-junker Oberfeldwebel Leo Schuhmacher at readiness on the wall behind the *Jagdverband's* dispersal hut at Munich-Riem, Feldwebel Josef 'Jupp' Dobnig (left) takes the opportunity to snack on some bread

engagement without result or loss to either side, while the other three took on bombers between Landshut and Erding.

One of these latter Me 262s was the A-1a/U4 with the long-barrelled Mauser 50 mm MK 214 cannon in its nose. Who was actually flying this aircraft remains unclear, but what is known is that it engaged B-26s of the 323rd and 344th BGs.

For their part, the crews of the 344th were very wary, for prior to the mission, they had been warned by their Wing HQ, 'This is a deep penetration into the "Redoubt" area. Be alert at all times for fighter interception. Two groups had brushes with Me 262s yesterday'.

Just before 1750 hrs, a single Me 262 was spotted by crews of the 323rd BG shadowing their formation, way out to the right, just after they had turned away from the target. It is probable that this was the Me 262 A-1a/U4. Its pilot initially circled around the third box of Marauders to make an attack from behind, closing in to about 500 yards, but without opening fire, before diving away to the right.

Capt John O Moench was flying as Group Lead with the 323rd BG. He remembered;

'Suddenly, the intercom came to life with the call out of fighters taking off from the Erding airfield below us. Almost instantly someone called out a fighter at "one o'clock". I looked up and well out in front of us, swinging around for what looked like a frontal attack, was an Me 262. As the enemy pilot turned, the 50 mm cannon sticking out of the nose of the Me 262 had the appearance of a giant telephone pole. Seconds later, the jet had passed well over the formation without firing a shot, well out of range of our 0.50-cal machine guns. Then we spotted him swinging around in a wide circle, seemingly to get into position to make another frontal pass. Again, he remained out of firing range and disappeared.

'Almost instantly, there was a call from the tail gunner that an Me 262 was off the rear. Crossing from the right, the jet swung around and came back from the left. Nineteen of the gunners opened up on it at maximum range and, apparently discouraged by the barrage of fire from the Marauders, the pilot broke off.'

Once again it seems that the 50 mm cannon in the A-1a/U4 had jammed or failed in some way – just as it had done when Herget had attempted to use it earlier in the month. There was some consolation for JV 44, however, when Unteroffizier Franz Köster, newly arrived from JG 7, shot down a P-51 and a P-38.

At dawn the next morning (26 April), JV 44 had 43 Me 262s on strength. Twelve of these aircraft would be despatched to engage more B-26 Marauders, this time from the 17th BG, which was out to bomb the recently evacuated jet base at Lechfeld and an ammunition dump at Schrobenhausen. They were part of a larger force from the USAAF's 42nd Bomb Wing, plus French Marauders. On this occasion, the JV 44 formation, which took off under grey skies just before 1130 hrs, was led by Galland himself. All the jets were armed with R4Ms, but as they climbed, one aircraft was forced to turn back because of an engine problem.

Thirty minutes later over Neuburg, the Germans spotted some 60 B-26s escorted by a similar number of P-47s. The 'mediums' had just aborted their bomb run due to the increasingly heavy cloud when JV 44's Me 262s closed in from head-on and then flashed over the bomber formation, before circling around and diving below the Marauders in order to attack them from below.

Unteroffizier Schallmoser, who had left hospital the day before despite his knee injury still troubling him, fired 'White 14's' R4Ms and watched as one B-26 exploded before him. The bomber's destruction may have been what 1Lt John W Sorrelle, piloting a B-26 of the 432nd BS, witnessed when he recalled;

'My tail gunner, TSgt Cleo E Wills, broke radio silence on the interphone. "Bandits coming out of the clouds at 'six o'clock low', climbing and closing fast. They look like '262s". I could feel my control column shuddering slightly as he began firing his twin 0.50-cal machine guns. The next events occurred in such rapid succession that I have no idea of the exact time sequence. "I got him! I got him!" Wills shouted over the intercom. Then the left wingman at my "ten o'clock" position exploded and was gone.'

One B-26 of the 432nd BS that was definitely struck by an R4M rocket was *Big Red*, piloted by 1Lt Alf P Shatto. The aircraft was left spinning out of control with its rear section very badly shot up and fuel streaming across the wings. Three crewmembers had been killed and the rest thrown out by the impact of the missile, as co-pilot 1Lt Charles E Bryner recorded;

'When the shell exploded, it disabled all the controls of our ship. I immediately ordered the crew to bail out, as the bomber was nosing upward very rapidly. I opened our bomb-bays and released our bomb load with the salvo switch. The bombardier, pilot and I were thrown out of the ship just 500 ft above the ground. The B-26 at this time was in a severe spin. Before our aircraft started downward in this spin, we were pinned down, unable to move, due to the centrifugal force, caused by the ship falling over on its back and going into a dive toward the ground.'

Fahnen-junker Oberfeldwebel Schuhmacher was not as fortunate as Schallmoser. Flying on what would be his only sortie with JV 44 against B-26s, he targeted one of the bombers, but found – much to his frustration – that his cannon had jammed. He was forced to fly through the enemy formation without firing a shot.

Flying a little above Schallmoser, Adolf Galland armed his Me 262's four MK 108s and flicked off the safety to the R4Ms. Already the Marauder tail gunners had opened fire at the approaching jets, and as he closed in, Galland selected as his target the outermost and rearmost B-26 of the first box. He depressed the rocket firing switch but nothing happened. Cursing, he realised that in the speed of his approach – just a matter of seconds – he had forgotten to flick off the second safety switch for the R4Ms, probably as a result of the distraction of the return fire.

Instinctively, he fired a burst from his cannon at a B-26, which erupted into flames and smoke, before passing right through the centre of the American formation and firing at another bomber. Around him, the waist gunners began to open fire at the speeding jet fighter, and very quickly Galland heard the dull thud of enemy shells striking his aircraft. The Messerschmitt began to trail smoke, but Galland was inquisitive about the fate of the second B-26, and as he left the bombers he banked his aircraft around to observe.

TSgt Henry Dietz was a gunner aboard the 17th BG's lead aircraft, flown by Capt Luther Gurkin, and he recalled;

The crew of Maj Luther Gurkin's B-26 Marauder of the 17th BG. Fourth from left in the crew line-up is gunner TSgt Henry Dietz, who is believed to have fired a burst at Adolf Galland's Me 262 as it passed his aircraft during the JV 44 attack against his formation over Bavaria on 26 April 1945. The damage was enough to slow Galland's jet down and leave it trailing smoke, thus setting it up as a target for escorting Thunderbolts

'Having been a weapons instructor, I naturally had a little experience with a 0.50-cal machine gun prior to "meeting" Generalleutnant Galland. Probably the most important thing I remembered from gunnery school was to fire short bursts and forget about the tracer bullets – just use your sights. That day, we were flying as flight leader, and we were about ten minutes from the target. I flew in the waist position from where I could see all mechanical parts of the aircraft. I had never seen a jet before. Galland slowed down to the speed of the B-26 so that he could observe and take score. I thought "Dummy"! He was flying low, right into the sights of my machine gun. I shot a burst. Nothing happened. A little higher, a little lower, I just kept shooting.'

Meanwhile, over the course of five firing passes, the Me 262s of JV 44 had inflicted carnage on other parts of the bomber formation, attacking from a bewildering number of angles and directions which taxed the American air gunners' skills to their limits. SSgt Bernard J Byrnes, a gunner aboard a B-26 of the 432nd BS, recalled;

'Our tail gunner, TSgt Jack Hogan, saw them first. They came up from below us and he fired the first shots from our flight. He held them off our own tail until they came up to the level of my gun turret and then I turned and started firing at a jet at about "seven o'clock", coming in high. All of a sudden I saw a big flash, and I turned the turret back to about "three o'clock", whereupon I realised that the other B-26 on the right side of us had gone. The Me 262 had blown it right out of the sky. He was still flying at our "three o'clock" position, and he was going after another B-26 in front of the one he had shot down. In this way, he made a perfect set-up for me. I was able to fire a long burst into him. His canopy was

1Lt James J Finnegan (left) of the 10th FS/50th FG poses with his crew chief on the cowling of his P-47D *The Irish Shillalah* at Giebelstadt for a snapshot in the spring of 1945. By firing a two-second burst at an Me 262 that had broken away from the attack on the 17th BG on 26 April, Finnegan is generally believed to have 'finished the job' started by TSgt Henry Dietz, and is credited with shooting down Generalleutnant Adolf Galland

badly damaged, and as he flipped over and away I thought I saw the canopy fly off, but I couldn't be sure.'

Any cohesion within the 17th BG's formation was lost, with only one of the group's four squadrons surviving without loss – and this despite the presence of four groups of fighter escort, one of which was to prove the nemesis to the commander of JV 44. Shortly after midday, P-47s of the 27th and 50th FGs came to the aid of the bombers, diving down from a higher altitude and firing their machine guns as they gave chase to the now quickly dispersing jets. The 50th FG had been detailed to escort the B-26s of the French 11e *Brigade de Bombardement*, and leading Green Flight of the 10th FS was 1Lt James J Finnegan. He remembered;

'I remember it well because it was the first time I saw operational jets. We had been briefed on them because they had been expected and used since October 1944. Yet, like a lot of intelligence we received in those times, nothing ever materialised.'

Finnegan was about to have a rude shock. Seconds earlier, he had watched in astonishment as two 'darts' streaked through the bomber formation just as two Marauders exploded in flames, at which point the 'darts' broke away to the left and right respectively.

'Somebody yelled "Jet Bandits!" over the intercom', Finnegan continued, 'and there was no doubt in my mind what they were – I had never seen anything move that fast.'

Finnegan watched the jet that had veered left, told his fellow pilots he was going after it and promptly rolled his P-47 on to its back and went into a 'split-S', holding the Me 262 in his gunsight. He fired a two-second burst at the enemy machine and observed strikes hitting the starboard side wing root. The jet banked sharply to the left and disappeared into clouds. Finnegan pulled away. 'I claimed an Me 262 as "damaged and probable" and thought no more of it'.

Adolf Galland recorded;

'A hail of fire enveloped me. A sharp rap hit my right knee, the instrument panel with its indispensable instruments was shattered, the right engine was also hit – its metal covering worked loose in the wind and was partly carried away – and now the left engine was hit. I could hardly hold her in the air.'

One-by-one the jets returned home, having claimed five B-26s, including one kill each for Unteroffizier Schallmoser and Feldwebel Kammerdiener. They were less two of their number, although one of the shot-down pilots had managed to bail out, and Kammerdiener's Messerschmitt had been hit in the right-hand engine, setting it on fire. His subsequent landing at Riem had proved difficult on one engine.

Following Kammerdiener in at around 1230 hrs was Adolf Galland, whose aircraft had been dealt a severe blow by Finnegan. His bullets had hit both the starboard engine as well as the port-side Jumo unit, which had sucked metal fragments into its manifold. Shells had also entered the cockpit from the rear, and as a result Galland now had to contend with the metal splinters which had embedded themselves in his knee and controls that no longer functioned.

'I had only one wish – to get out of this "crate", which now apparently was only good for dying in', he subsequently wrote. 'But then I was paralysed by the terror of being shot while parachuting down. Experience had taught us that we jet fighter pilots had to reckon on this. I soon discovered that after some adjustments, my battered Me 262 could be steered again and, after a dive through the layer of cloud, I saw the

An Me 262 is caught on gun camera film by a pursuing American fighter. This still probably shows a scene similar to the moment when Generalleutnant Galland attempted to land his damaged jet at Munich-Riem on 26 April 1945

Autobahn below me. Ahead lay Munich and to the left, Riem. In a few seconds I was over the airfield. Having regained my self-confidence, I gave the customary wing wobble and started banking to come in. It was remarkably quiet and dead below. One engine did not react at all to the throttle, and as I could not reduce it, I had to cut both engines just before the edge of the airfield. A long trail of smoke drifted behind me.'

The Me 262 bumped to a halt with a flat tyre as Galland threw open the canopy and clambered out awkwardly, just as Allied fighter-bombers had begun a strafing run over Riem. He was about to fall into the 'shelter' of a bomb-crater when he was welcomed by a timely mechanic riding a semi-tracked *Kettenkrad* tow vehicle. The Generalleutnant limped gratefully over to it and the little vehicle rumbled off to safety, with Galland trembling and shocked on the rear seat.

Like Steinhoff, Schallmoser and other members of his unit, Galland was packed off to hospital, where he received X-rays to his wounded knee. He later recorded the aftermath of what would be his last combat mission;

'Since it was impossible to remove two of the steel fragments from my knee, it was put into plaster – otherwise, I would have been confined to a hospital bed. The plaster was therefore preferable. Although my own operative flying had come to an abrupt end, the history of my unit was to continue.'

The ground staff of JV 44 found conditions equally hazardous. In late April, Obersting. Frodl, a technical officer who had been transferred from JG 7, was injured during a low-level fighter attack on Riem as he attempted to reach the cover of buildings at the edge of the airfield on a 750 cc BMW motorcycle, rather than diving into a one-man foxhole. Despite suffering broken bones, he managed to ride the motorcycle to a temporary field hospital, before being moved to Oberföhring for more permanent treatment.

While Galland languished in plaster, at 1800 hrs on the 26th, JV 44 was reporting 31 Me 262s on strength (including the aircraft arrived from *Stab*, I., II. and IV./KG 51), of which only nine were serviceable.

General Koller, however, had different figures, and fumed in his diary;

'*Jagdverband* 44 reports 95 Me 262s on its airfield in Munich, but can only cope with 25 because of insufficient personnel. That is unheard of. In other words, there are 70 Me 262s standing around uselessly in Riem, and JG 7, which has sunk to 20 aircraft, requires reinforcements most urgently. Find out who has allowed the aircraft to accumulate there – Kammler, Kammhuber, Saur? Each will blame the other, but we will institute court martial proceedings for sabotage against whoever is guilty. We have to allow ourselves to be insulted continuously, and these "Plenipotentiaries" mess around like a bunch of lunatics let loose. The 70 aircraft, or as many as are serviceable, are to be sent to JG 7 immediately. Get the Quartermaster-General to work on it.'

One reason so many jet aircraft were 'standing around' at Riem was probably because of the relatively comfortable fuel stocks still available there. On the evening of the 26th, the Quartermaster General reported 141 cubic metres of J2 fuel at Munich – substantially more than many of the other main jet airfields, but still less than at Prague (243 cubic metres), and Lechfeld, which had just been evacuated, and which still held 218 cubic metres!

The worsening situation on the ground gave rise to a fresh set of knee-jerk orders. At midnight, OKL warned regional Luftwaffe commands about the possibility of an Allied threat to the Czech Protectorate from Passau. In such a case, German forces were to 'split and spread south'. JV 44 was to make its Me 262s available to offer close-support for the ground units – a clear indication that it was to join the piston-engine day fighter *Gruppen* which were bombing and strafing Allied columns in the Passau area.

Adolf Galland's injury forced a change in the operational leadership of JV 44. Although he would remain ultimately in command from his temporary headquarters in a commandeered forester's lodge – and indeed would issue some dramatic orders in the coming days – it would be Heinz Bär who, at this point, assumed day-to-day control of the tactical operations of the *Verband*. Galland's decision was based on the fact that Bär was probably the most experienced jet pilot in southern Germany, and he had expressed a firm desire to continue operations. Galland admitted to one historian;

'Herget was now with me as my Offizier z.b.V., Steinhoff was badly burnt and was in hospital, Barkhorn had been injured following his bad landing in an Me 262 and Krupinski did not have the experience that Bär had.'

On 27 April, Heinz Bär, flying the Me 262 A-1/U5 six-MK 108 prototype, led what was possibly his first sortie with JV 44 when, accompanied by Major Herget and Unteroffizier Köster, he engaged American fighters over Riem. Each of the three pilots claimed an enemy fighter shot down.

With Galland wounded, Steinhoff severely burned and Lützow missing, Galland appointed Oberstleutnant Heinz Bär to take acting command of JV 44. He is seen here at Munich-Riem (centre) with, to left, Major Erich Hohagen (hand in jacket) and, to right, Hauptmann Walter Krupinski

While not in the air, it seems most of Bär's time was spent giving hasty instruction to the new pilots still being assigned to JV 44. Fähnrich Gerhard Frisch, a pilot with I./JG 2 who had been instructed to join the '*Kampfgruppe Galland* somewhere around Augsburg and Lechfeld', eventually arrived at Riem. Having reported to Bär, he was given two hours training before going solo on the Me 262 over Riem.

The following morning, telex orders arrived at Feldkirchen from Generalmajor Friedrich Kless, the Chief of Staff of *Luftflottenkommando* 6, instructing JV 44 to make urgent preparations to move east to Hörsching, near Linz, in Austria. From here it was intended to use the *Verband* on ground-support missions and against enemy fighter-bombers operating ahead of the expected Allied thrust against the Passau-Linz area. The unit was to move there with all its groundcrew, mechanics, armourers and technicians.

However, during a telephone discussion with Kless, Galland dismissed such an idea on the grounds that the air control and ground support infrastructure at Hörsching was inadequate to meet the needs of his *Verband*. Furthermore, weather conditions in the mountainous transfer area were not good, making it too risky for the movement of an entire flying unit.

It was agreed instead that, owing to 'enemy pressure', JV 44 would move to Salzburg-Maxglan, via specially prepared and camouflaged dispersal facilities off the Munich-Salzburg Autobahn in the Hofoldinger Forest and temporary landing strips along the Autobahn itself, which were to be available for operations within two days. The ultimate destination

Me 262s parked in woods off the side of an Autobahn somewhere in southern Germany. On 28 April 1945, further to discussions between Galland and the Chief-of-Staff of *Luftflottenkommando* 6, JV 44 received orders to prepare to operate from such facilities in the Hofoldinger Forest, south of Munich

A view purportedly showing an Me 262 flown – at one time at least while he was with III./EJG 2 – by Major Erich Hohagen, and later abandoned at the side of an Autobahn in southern Germany, not far from Lechfeld

An Me 262 lies abandoned and stripped of its engines and wheels at the side of an Autobahn

for the unit, however, was to be Innsbruck, to where JV 44 would also send all Me 262s which had been undergoing repair and maintenance at the Deutsche Lufthansa hangars at Riem.

Orders were issued for the pilots and groundcrews of JV 44 to pack their personal belongings and equipment and prepare to load them onto military lorries that would transport them to the next operational base the following day. Together with some non-flying comrades, Feldwebel Josef Dobnig rode a bicycle several kilometres to the home of the wife of a local soldier to help ferry some items of luggage for safe-keeping.

The transfer of aircraft started quickly, with small numbers of Me 262s being flown out of Riem to Neubiberg, from where the aircraft were towed by *Kettenkrads* into woods or even barns.

Meanwhile, Adolf Galland experienced the first in a set of extraordinary events that were to take place over the coming days. During the late afternoon of 28 April, he received visits from SS-*Obergruppenführer* Kammler and Generalmajor Kammhuber, acting as 'Plenipotentiaries' for Hitler and (the now disgraced) Göring, respectively. The city of Munich had experienced rumblings of 'rebellion' from an independently-minded Catholic group known as the 'Free Bavaria' movement, which had set about preparing to take control of the city from its Nazi overlords in the hours before the anticipated arrival of the Americans.

With one boot casually resting on an abandoned bomb, and clad in the typical flying clothing of the time, Feldwebel Josef 'Jupp' Dobnig (formerly a fighter instructor with JG 103) is photographed quickly eating a sandwich while standing alongside the wall that ran immediately behind JV 44's dispersal hut at Munich-Riem in April 1945. He was the last JV 44 pilot to leave Riem – but it would not be in an aircraft

Somehow word had got out to the military command that Galland may have thrown in his lot with the 'rebels' and offered them the services of his valuable Me 262s. Kammler and Kammhuber had decided that it would be best to move JV 44 north, to Prague, rather than into Austria. However, when the 'Plenipotentiaries' observed a weary and irritated Galland with his right leg encased in plaster, they extended their sympathies and bade him farewell!

Shortly after their departure, Galland left his accommodation and relocated south to Bad Wiessee with his personal staff, comprising Hauptmann Hugo Kessler as his adjutant and Major Herget as his Officer for Special Tasks. Herget would be needed to carry out Galland's last, and probably most audacious, initiative of the war. At Bad Wiessee, Galland joined up once more with 'Macki' Steinhoff, who was still receiving treatment for his burns.

In the meantime, Feldwebel Dobnig returned to Riem on his bicycle to discover to his dismay that the first of JV 44's jets was already airborne, en route for Austria, and that American advance units had reached the western and northern outskirts of Munich. Riding over to JV 44's dispersal area, he found the place cleared of virtually all equipment and personnel except for a Luftwaffe technical officer, a hangar foreman and a mechanic, who were loading some last pieces of equipment on to a lorry.

The Luftwaffe officer hurriedly ordered Dobnig to fly the sole remaining airworthy Me 262 at Munich-Riem to Innsbruck, where he could join other elements of JV 44. A somewhat bewildered Dobnig dutifully went to climb into the aircraft, but as he did so, the hangar foreman ran up and warned him that the jet fighter was not fit to fly as it was suffering from undercarriage retraction problems.

Dobnig looked at the Me 262 and realised that even if he did use it to fly to Innsbruck, in its condition it would be in no position to take on any Allied fighters he may encounter en route, and it would also burn more precious fuel. The foreman quietly suggested to Dobnig that it would be safer for him to accompany the three of them as far as Salzburg, and to re-join the main elements of JV 44 there. Dobnig willingly loaded his bicycle and his rucksack with personal belongings onto the lorry and, a short while later, the last members of JV 44 evacuated Munich-Riem.

The lone Me 262 seen in the line-up of abandoned aircraft at Riem in the photograph on page 38. It is possible that this was the defective aircraft that 'Jupp' Dobnig was ordered to fly out of Munich on or around 28 April 1945. The aircraft is finished in the dark green overspray seen on several of JV 44's jets

RED AND WHITE RIDDLE

It may have been a technologically superior aircraft and it may have been a first-rate interceptor, but the Me 262 was not without its weaknesses. In its early operations, the aircraft's twin Jumo 004 turbojets and its nosewheel proved unreliable. The former was susceptible to flame-outs and malfunction, while the latter was prone to flutter and shimmy and, quite frequently, collapse – especially on rubble-littered and cratered runways.

Later, many pilots found the Me 262's 'dogfighting' capabilities severely compromised because of its poor turning radius. But perhaps most dangerous of all were the vulnerable moments when an Me 262 prepared to take off or when it approached for landing.

At such moments, greater lengths of time and distance were needed than for conventional fighter aircraft. The Me 262 also required a longer period of time to start its engines, and this would frequently have to be done in the open, thus exposing the aircraft to the very real threat of attack from increasingly numerous and ever-confident Allied fighters. The risk at Munich-Riem in April 1945 was particularly acute due to the large numbers of Me 262s now gathered there.

The logical, though somewhat resource-inefficient, solution was to provide aerial protection to the jets at these dangerous moments. At Riem, Galland opted to use the Focke-Wulf Fw 190D variant for such a role – the interim high-altitude interceptor fitted with a 1770 hp Jumo 213 engine, which gave the fighter its distinctive, sleek 'long-nose' appearance. Walter Krupinski recalled;

'The problem for us was that every time we took off and landed, there were enemy fighter aircraft active either very near to us or actually over the field. The front was just on the other side of Munich, and as a result of this situation an idea was born to form a special unit to protect us. You couldn't do much with an Me 262 on a landing pass – you had very low speed and if you tried to accelerate, you needed too much time. It was a time when we were at our most vulnerable. So came the idea to use the Fw 190D-9s.'

A small number of such machines was assembled under the command of Knight's Cross-holder Leutnant Heinz Sachsenberg. Flying, it could be said, was in 'Heino' Sachsenberg's blood, for he was the son of a World War 1 *Pour le Mérite* holder and later director of the Junkers aircraft company, while his brother had flown nightfighters.

A native of Dessau, his first operational posting was with 6./JG 52 in the East in 1942. He was awarded the Knight's Cross for his 101st victory on 9 June 1944, but was severely wounded in August that year during operations over Rumania. Sachsenberg would end the war with 500 missions and 104 victories to his credit. Walter Krupinski remembered

Striking a statuesque pose, Leutnant Heinz Sachsenberg, the nominal commander of JV 44's semi-autonomous airfield defence flight, studies the cowling of one of his *Schwarm's* Fw 190D-9s

Four pilots of the JV 44
Platzschutzschwarm gather
for a photograph in front of an
Fw 190D-9 at Ainring in May 1945.
They are, from left to right, Leutnant
Karl-Heinz Hofmann, Leutnant Heinz
Sachsenberg, Hauptmann Waldemar
Wübke and Oberleutnant
Klaus Faber

him as having an attitude that was 'crazy', while a fellow pilot who would fly Fw 190s with him while with JV 44 recalled that he would fight as long as he had fuel and ammunition. One of the pilots who flew protection sorties under Sachsenberg at Munich-Riem remembered that his method of formal instruction constituted standing on the wing of a Focke-Wulf as it taxied at high-speed in order to convince himself that the pilot had adequate control of his aircraft!

The most reliable documentary evidence indicates that five Fw 190Ds were attached to JV 44 in what was the unit's *Platzschutzschwarm* (Airfield Defence Flight), although it cannot be ruled out that there were more. Strangely, the handful of pilots who made up the *Schwarm* led a very autonomous existence. Indeed, apart from the occasional meal together at Feldkirchen (although dining at the same table, they would apparently sit apart from the jet pilots), they had little contact with the nucleus of their parent unit's pilots, being accommodated separately in a farmhouse to the north of the airfield in which they shared rooms. And the circumstances in which each pilot was assigned to JV 44 was somewhat unconventional, even by that stage of the war.

Oberleutnant Klaus Faber was an experienced fighter pilot who had served with JG 27 and JG 5. He had suffered a landing accident in North Africa while with JG 27, and after recuperating from his injuries, served for a time as a navigational instructor, before being posted to *Stab/*JG 6 and serving with Gerhard Barkhorn. In April 1945, however, Faber was unexpectedly ordered to Obertraubling, where, on behalf of *General der Jagdflieger* Oberst Gollob, he was to collect an Fw 190 and fly it to Munich-Riem, where he was to report to JV 44.

Joining Faber from JG 6 was Feldwebel Bodo Dirschauer, who had had a very varied service career in which he had flown Bf 109s in Russia with JG 52, before being assigned to KG 26 to fly torpedo-bomber operations. Wounded over the Baltic, Dirschauer was hospitalised, but he discharged himself and was posted to 3./JG 5, which was redesignated 11./JG 6, where he served under Faber.

In late 1944, Dirschauer was posted to III./EJG 2 at Lechfeld in order to undergo conversion to the Me 262, but on 12 April 1945 he was ordered to board a Si 204 destined for Riem. As soon as he landed there, Dirschauer was instructed to make his way to a wooden hut on the northern side of the airfield, which served as Sachsenberg's 'headquarters'. Here Dirschauer observed a small number of Fw 190s pushed backed into primitive blast shelters under the cover of trees at the edge of the airfield. These had been constructed by local auxiliary troops. Walter Krupinski remembered;

'They were based very near to us – parked on the northern edge of the airfield and hidden in trees. They came out when we were due to start, and we felt very safe when we were getting airborne or landing knowing they were there. It was a good idea of Galland's to have those Focke-Wulfs there.'

Four days after Dirschauer joined the *Platzschutzschwarm*, Sachsenberg was further reinforced by the arrival of ex-EJG 2 instructor Leutnant Karl-Heinz Hofmann and veteran pilot Hauptmann Waldemar Wübke, who had initially been posted to JG 54 in 1940. Wounded twice with this unit, Wübke's injuries eventually took him away from frontline service, and he assumed command of fighter training unit II./JG 101. When that

Leutnant Heinz Sachsenberg (far left) smiles down at the camera while sat alongside fellow pilots from his *Platzschutzschwarm* on the cowling of Fw 190D-9 'Red 3' at Ainring in May 1945. These men are, from left to right, Hauptmann Waldemar Wübke (next to Sachsenberg), Oberleutnant Klaus Faber and Leutnant Karl-Heinz Hofmann

Gruppe was disbanded in mid-April 1945, he was sent to JV 44. Initially, it was intended that Wübke should fly the Me 262, but after a short while he joined Sachsenberg.

Within a short period of time, so it would seem, the *Doras* of the *Platzschutzschwarm* were brought up to readiness and flew their first covering flights. By the evening of 23 April, JV 44 reported five Fw 190D-9/11s on strength, but only two aircraft were serviceable.

At least three of the Focke-Wulfs are known to have been D-9s, while one, Wk-Nr. 170933?, coded 'Red 4', was a D-11. Its origins are believed to be with the *Verbandsführerschule General der Jagdflieger* (General of Fighter's Unit Leaders School) at Bad Wörishofen, which presumably had a past affiliation with Adolf Galland, or which, under Gollob's instruction, released the aircraft to JV 44.

Tactics were simple. Flights were to be undertaken in two-aircraft *Rotte* up to an altitude of 460 metres, all the while keeping eyes on both the Me 262s taking off or landing and the surrounding skies over Riem for enemy fighters. Sachsenberg also gave strict orders that his pilots were neither to break off from their 'chained dog' mission or to attempt to fly alongside the jets.

One difficulty that the *Platzschutzschwarm* pilots immediately encountered was that in order to give the Me 262s a clear landing approach, they had to land before the jets returned from a sortie, thus

Fw 190D-9 Wk-Nr. 600424 'Red 1' of JV 44's *Platzschutzschwarm*, photographed at Munich-Riem after the cessation of hostilities. Behind it is another view of the unit's Si 204 'White 63'. Note the severely damaged control tower in the background

The motif below the cockpit of Fw 190D-9 'Red 1' read *'Verkaaft's mei Gwand 'I foahr in himmel!'* ('Sell my clothes, I'm going to heaven'). Note the makeshift wheeled support placed under the tail assembly – probably necessary as a result of damage to, or the collapse of, the tailwheel

Right and below right
Two views of Fw 190D-9 Wk-Nr. 600424 'Red 1', showing to advantage the distinctive red and white striped undersides common to the aircraft of the JV 44 *Platzschutzschwarm*. This marking was intended as a means of quick identification for the unit's Me 262 pilots as they took off and landed – their most vulnerable moments. It also served to warn airfield flak batteries that the Fw 190Ds were friendly, and therefore not to be shot at!

Below
Fw 190D-9 'Red 3' at Ainring. The front of the spinner was painted yellow, with the rear section in black. Throughout the war, Ainring had been used as an aeronautical test centre and by Hitler and Göring during visits to Berchtesgaden

nullifying any offer of protection. Ground control would give them clearance to land, but there was no radio contact between the Me 262s and the Fw 190s.

Feldwebel Dirschauer apparently flew some 12 protection flights over Riem, including three on one day in mid-April. Adolf Galland recalled;

'The Americans were constantly observing our airfields, and they attacked anybody who came out or who tried to get in, especially at Munich-Riem once they knew we were there. We lost some of our men that way. Sachsenberg was a good pilot, and we felt safer when his aircraft were in the air. They surrounded the airfield – not in any formation – but usually just in pairs. We tried to get them into the air just as we took off and also when we came in to land, but often it didn't work because conditions were becoming impossible both on the airfield and in the air. Once up, they escorted us around the airfield. With our undercarriages up and the jets climbing away, it was time for the Fw 190Ds to come back.'

On at least one occasion, it is known that the Focke-Wulfs engaged P-47s in combat over Riem while flying a cover sortie for the Me 262s.

As a measure intended to offer clear identification of its friendly, low-flying piston-engine aircraft to both the Me 262 pilots and the wary flak batteries at Riem, JV 44 introduced a very unique recognition feature which has, in recent years, provided considerable interest and debate among Luftwaffe researchers.

Although it remains unclear who originated such a directive, orders were nevertheless issued to paint the undersides of each Focke-Wulf

One for the album. Knight's Cross-holder Leutnant Heinz Sachsenberg grins broadly for the camera, while the other three members of the JV 44 *Platzschutzschwarm* (from left to right), Leutnant Karl-Heinz Hofmann, Hauptmann Waldemar Wübke and Oberleutnant Klaus Faber, seem more contemplative. Note the thick mud of Ainring airfield coating both Sachsenberg's boots and the starboard mainwheel of Fw 190 D-9 'Red 3' – evidence of spring rainfall

Fw 190D-9 Wk-Nr. 213240 'Red 13' of *Jagdverband* 44 is used as a 'prop' by US troops as they pose for a snapshot at Ainring in late May 1945

bright red with unevenly spaced white stripes of varying widths. This, combined with the individual pilots' mottos, yellow spinners and unusual segmented *Schwarm* emblems painted beneath the cockpit of each aircraft, made these machines very distinctive.

At 1800 hrs on 26 April, JV 44 still reported five Fw 190D-9/11s on its strength, but it is worth recalling that this was the day Galland landed his shot-up jet at Riem in the midst of an Allied strafing attack. The *Platzschutzschwarm* seems to have been mysteriously absent.

As the American advance closed in on Munich, on 27 April JV 44 prepared to relocate its jets east to Salzburg, while the *Platzschutzschwarm*

Fw 190D-9 Wk-Nr. 213240 'Red 13' sits abandoned at Ainring with only Bf 109Gs from II./JG 52 for company

flew some of its aircraft to the airfield at Ainring, just to the west of that city (see Chapter Five). However, at least two Fw 190Ds remained at Riem (probably abandoned due to technical defects or lack of spare parts, and showing signs of damage), and these relatively intact fighters were discovered by US forces when they captured the airfield.

Whatever the case, the story of the *Platzschutzschwarm* provides a colourful distraction from JV 44's core jet operations. Little information is available as to the scale of the *Schwarm's* activities, or its effectiveness while at Riem, and, to date, there are few accounts which testify to any coordinated form of operations between the Fw 190Ds and the Me 262s.

A view of the starboard side of Fw 190D-9 Wk-Nr. 213240 'Red 13'. The aircraft incorporated an early style canopy, which was possibly a replacement

MOUNTAIN KINGS

L ate April 1945 saw American forces thrust deeper and deeper into southern Germany. Generally, they encountered scant resistance, the infantry and armour of the US Seventh Army racing through the valleys of Bavaria and along the Autobahn toward Munich. On the 28th, Generalleutnant Galland decided that the time had come to evacuate Riem and relocate JV 44's Me 262s to the airfield at Maxglan, some three kilometres southwest of Salzburg, in Austria, while those Fw 190Ds of the *Platzschutzschwarm* which he had not ordered to be destroyed were to go to Ainring.

OKL had already – and somewhat optimistically – designated Salzburg-Maxglan as 'an alternative airfield from which (jet) aircraft can take off again with tanks half full and/or with rocket assistance'. Although there was a concrete runway here, and supplies of the necessary J2 fuel were rushed in, in comparison to Munich-Riem, conditions at Maxglan were rather primitive.

The first formation of Me 262s (which is known to have included Oberfeldwebel Nielinger in 'White 12') flew out of Riem during the early afternoon of the 28th and made course for Salzburg, flying over Rosenheim, the Chiemsee and Traunstein, before arriving at Maxglan 22 minutes later. The jet pilots had to endure two dangers as they came in – firstly, they had to throttle back to avoid low-slung power cables at the northern edge of the airfield, and secondly, as they approached, the local flak batteries opened fire on them.

As one of the Me 262s landed and drew to a stop on the runway, its anxious pilot leapt from the cockpit and fired his recognition flares in an attempt to cease the guns. He was successful, and fortunately none of the

Me 262 'White 12' of JV 44 lies with its inspection panels missing and collapsed mainwheels at Innsbruck-Hötting

aircraft fell to 'friendly fire', although one Me 262 ('White 22') slithered into a pile of gravel near the edge of the runway and lay abandoned there until the arrival of US forces.

Adverse weather prevented a second formation following, and further departure was delayed until the next morning, when Oberstleutnant Bär led a group which left Riem at intervals between 0800 and 0930 hrs. It included Unteroffizier Müller, Feldwebel Kammerdiener, Unteroffizier Schallmoser and Feldwebel Steiner.

Other pilots that are known to have assembled at Salzburg-Maxglan included Major Hohagen, Hauptmann Krupinski, Leutnant Fährmann, Leutnant Neumann, Leutnant Stigler, Fahnen-junker Oberfeldwebel Schuhmacher and Oberfeldwebel Knier. Among the last personnel to leave Munich were Hauptmann Gutowski, Major Schnell and Fahnen-junker Oberfeldwebel Kaiser, who emptied the operations room at Feldkirchen and left it to the new occupiers – conscripted Polish labourers, who were employed to carry out repairs and maintenance at Riem. Gutowski and his colleagues journeyed to Salzburg by road with a small cadre of mechanics and armourers from JV 44.

Above and right
Me 262 'White 22' nosed into a pile of gravel at the edge of the runway at Salzburg-Maxglan as the first element of JV 44 transferred there from Munich-Riem on 28 April 1945

Not all of JV 44's Me 262s made it to Salzburg or Innsbruck. Here, Wk-Nr. 111074 is pictured abandoned in the Hofoldinger Forest. It appears as if the aircraft has been deliberately damaged with an explosive charge of some kind at the join between the fuselage and the tail assembly, and that the Jumo 004 engine nacelles have been damaged with a hammer, or been driven in to. Note that the nosewheel towbar has been left fixed to the wheel – evidence of hurried action

The remainder of the ground-crews were to prepare to transfer to Bad Aibling, along with jet aircraft spare parts and other equipment, where they were to await further orders for onward movement to Innsbruck.

On 29 April it seems there was an attempt to introduce some cohesion into the scattered remnants of the Luftwaffe's jet fighter force by redesignating JV 44 as the new IV./JG 7 – also to be known as the *'Gefechtsverband Galland'* (Combat Group Galland) under the command of IX. *Fliegerkorps*, and with a list strength of 25 aircraft. The *Verband* was to hand any of its aircraft considered to be 'surplus' (possibly those machines formerly with KG 51) over to JG 7, which was in the process of relocating to Prague.

Meanwhile, JV 44 began setting up at Maxglan. Several of the unit's pilots found accommodation in a disused Labour Service camp near to the airfield, while the jets were pushed back into a camouflaged dispersal area in woods to the southwestern edge of the airfield in the Scherzerwald and Eichetwald. Operating the Me 262 from Maxglan was to prove very difficult, as the take-off run, which was to have been undertaken from north to south, was extremely limited – so limited, in fact, that just one combat sortie is known to have been attempted. This also took place on the 29th, when Oberstleutnant Bär apparently took off in an Me 262 and shot down a P-47 near Bad Aibling.

That evening, IX. *Fliegerkorps* signalled Bär demanding to know why no Me 262s had arrived at Prague. It is not known if Bär gave a response, but the following day nine jets from KG 51 did go there.

Four-and-a-half kilometres to the west, just over the Saalach, Leutnant Sachsenberg, Oberleutnant Faber, Hauptmann Wübke and Leutnant Hofmann flew the Fw 190Ds of JV 44's *Platzschutzschwarm* into Ainring. Stretching across a picturesque valley, the grass-strip airfield enjoyed magnificent views towards Bad Reichenhall and Berchtesgaden, as well as the foothills of the Alps. Hitler and Göring used the airfield when visiting Berchtesgaden, and it had also functioned as a gliding and general aeronautical test centre.

When Sachsenberg and his fellow pilots climbed out of their Focke-Wulfs, they found themselves surrounded by an eclectic collection of aircraft, including DFS 250 gliders, the He 280 V7 that had been used for motorless gliding experiments, a Ju 88 fitted to carry a V1 flying bomb and the unusual twin-rotor Focke-Achgelis Fa 223 helicopters of *Transportstaffel* 40.

It seems the *Platzschutzschwarm* engaged in little aerial activity of any consequence from Ainring, although what communications existed – if any – with its parent unit at Maxglan is not known. On the second or third day of May, however, Klaus Faber took off in 'Red 13' on a courier flight for Bad Aibling. En route, he encountered some P-47s and P-51s on a fighter sweep. Alone, and with 'reckless abandon', he attacked the American fighters and is reputed to have claimed two P-47s shot down.

The situation was somewhat bleak for those members of JV 44 who may have reached Bad Aibling. The airfield commander there apparently had just 13 rifles to hand out to the 5000-odd men who had turned up there in recent days. 'We can choose a spot in the woods and wait there with our white flag until the American tanks get through', he told a senior German officer. 'There's nothing else we can do'.

But at Salzburg on 30 April, orders were received from *Luftflottenkommando* 6 to the effect that any aircraft not directly associated with jet operations were to clear the field to enable it to be used 'exclusively' by Me 262s. There also seemed to be a general drift by certain Luftwaffe commands into the area as the Allied advance pressed further south.

Elements of the staff of IX. *Fliegerkorps* prepared to move to Bad Aibling as an interim measure, before making a wholesale move of the command to Hörsching. This may have been indicative of the intention to prepare for a retreat to the so-called 'Alpine Redoubt', the anticipated mountain 'citadel' from where senior Nazis were planning to fight a last-ditch, guerrilla-style final campaign to the last man. More realistic minds viewed this plan as fantasy, as *General der Flieger* Karl Koller, the Luftwaffe Chief-of-Staff, scoffed in his diary;

'OKW Staff South is issuing orders on the Alps Fortress. Only combat troops and command staffs are supposed to go into the Alps – all other units are to remain outside. Supplies are to be improved. In addition, industrial plants for the manufacture of ammunition are to be erected. Saur or Kammler is even thinking of starting up aircraft plants (that's all nonsense). All too many non-combat troops and obsolete rear-echelon units have already penetrated the Alps. It is impossible to get them out again. There is sufficient food for three weeks.

'The fortress has in no way been prepared – no fortifications, no guns. The equipment of the troops now entering the fortress is completely unsuitable for mountain warfare. For the most part mobile units, they will be completely crippled once the big North-South valley roads and the big East-West road in the Innsbruck-Lent Valley have been destroyed by the enemy air force.'

The scene awaiting American troops at Ainring in May 1945. Fw 190D-9 Wk-Nr. 213240 'Red 13' of the JV 44 *Platzschutzschwarm* (one of three such aircraft found there) is surrounded by Bf 109s of II./JG 52

Into the atmosphere of orders and counter-orders which surrounded JV 44 came Major Hans-Ekkehard Bob, a very highly regarded fighter pilot and unit commander, and a holder of the Knight's Cross with 59 victories. Bob was both a man who lived for flight and a true Luftwaffe veteran, having joined JG 334 as a young Oberfähnrich in late 1935. He first saw operations during the occupation of the Sudetenland flying Ar 68 biplanes (without ammunition) as 'escort' to German transports and bombers.

After being assigned to I./JG 21 for the invasion of Poland, this *Gruppe* was redesignated III./JG 54 for the French campaign in May 1940 and Bob later fought over Dunkirk, where his first victories were over RAF Gloster Gladiators. During the Battle of Britain, Bob led the Bf 109Es of 9./JG 54 on almost daily sorties over the British Isles, either on freelance fighter sweeps or as escort to bombers, before experimenting in fighter-bomber operations in September of that year by using single 250-kg bombs slung under the Bf 109's fuselage in several successful missions against London. Awarded the Knight's Cross in May 1941 following his 19th victory, Bob was then sent to Russia to fly fighter missions over the advance on Leningrad.

In June 1943, he left JG 54 to take up a new position as *Kommandeur* of IV./JG 51, but Bob was transferred again in August 1944 when he took command of II./JG 3. Its Bf 109Gs had been rushed from the Reich to the Normandy invasion, where the unit fought a battle of attrition against the Allies. Just a month later, however, Bob was transferred yet again, this time to the newly formed *Erprobungskommando Lechfeld*, where, due to chronic fuel shortages, he received just two hours of rudimentary training on the Me 262.

At the beginning of 1945, he was ordered to Berlin, where he joined a small team of experienced officers assigned to the staff of Generalmajor Kammhuber in his capacity as the *Reichsmarschall's* Plenipotentiary for Jet Aircraft. For a while Bob worked on the staff directly responsible for allocation of newly built Me 262s, before being ordered by Kammhuber to Silesia, where, due to his piloting skills, he joined I. and II./EJG 2, both these units being responsible for the conversion training of former bomber pilots onto single-engine fighters. Bob's peacetime training on multi-engine aircraft, and his experience in blind-flying, made him an ideal instructor, sympathetic to the bomber men's training needs.

In late April 1945, however, the Russian advance into Silesia brought an end to EJG 2's activities there, and Bob received orders to transfer to Munich-Riem and report for duty with Oberstleutnant Bär and JV 44. Reaching Riem from Silesia via a crippled transport network took time, and Bob finally arrived at the airport around 30 April, only to discover that Bär had left for Salzburg and Galland was absent.

Having been there for a only a few hours, he contacted Kammhuber's local representative, Stuka pilot Major Werner Roell, who instructed him to proceed 'immediately' to Innsbruck, where he was to make preparations for the arrival of a group of Me 262s from JV 44 which was expected to transfer there imminently. This instruction originated in a proposal to Kammhuber by Galland on 28 April as a counterplan to sending Me 262s to Prague.

By coincidence, a number of Me 262s that were not officially on the strength of JV 44 were already at Riem undergoing work in the *Deutsche*

Major Hans-Ekkehard Bob joined JV 44 during the final days of the war, and he was despatched to Innsbruck to coordinate the arrival of an element of the unit's Me 262s at Hötting airfield. Bob had been awarded the Knight's Cross in May 1941, and ended the war with 59 victories, including the destruction of a B-17 with which he collided

Lufthansa workshops. Galland suggested that these aircraft be flown to Innsbruck – a less 'risky' destination – by any remaining jet-qualified pilots still available at Riem. Interim ground support was to be provided by personnel from I./KG(J) 54.

Unable to procure an aircraft, despite his status, Bob was forced to drive to Innsbruck. When he got there he found conditions woefully inadequate for the task. Although there were two airfields available, he discarded the old civilian aerodrome since the dispersal facilities were not sufficient and the runway was too short. At Hötting there was another field located just north of the River Inn that had been laid out more recently, and which featured a grass strip of some 800 metres. This was still too short, but as Bob recalled;

'There was neither adequate accommodation, nor splinter-proof standings, nor food, nor ammunition, nor the necessary J2 fuel needed for jet fighters. The landing strip was too short, as the Me 262 needed about 1200 metres for take-off on grass. I reported all this to Munich-Riem and was ordered to arrange for an adequate extension of the landing strip. The work was eventually done using the services of a labour service unit acting under orders of the airfield commander.'

By 1 May, collapse of the entire German military and political infrastructure seemed imminent. The Americans had reached the northern outskirts of Munich. In Berlin, Adolf Hitler, *Führer* of the Thousand Year Reich, had shot himself. Hermann Göring, ostensibly still Commander-in-Chief of the Luftwaffe, was under house arrest in a castle near Salzburg.

In northern Germany, Montgomery's 21st Army Group was advancing virtually unopposed towards the Baltic Sea. In Italy, where more secret talks instigated by the SS had been conducted with American forces with a view to achieving a negotiated surrender, the front had finally collapsed. An ambiguously worded message had gone out from Bormann – still deep in the Berlin bunker – to Admiral Dönitz, appointing him Hitler's successor as *Führer* in accordance with Hitler's revised testament. But Dönitz was hesitant to assume control of what was now left of the Third Reich.

Meanwhile, *Luftflottenkommando* 6 declared in a signal that Generalleutnant Galland had been placed under its command, while JV 44's aircraft were now to come under the direction of IX. *Fliegerkorps*, along with all other jet units still operating. There was a suggestion that the unit could also relocate to Hörsching at some stage, but for the time being it was to continue to fly defensive sorties against the enemy advance from the west. The reality was that JV 44 had effectively ceased flying operational sorties – its new airfields were not yet geared up sufficiently to support full-scale combat operations.

It is unlikely if these events and instructions were known to Adolf Galland – and even if they were, there was little he could do, should he have cared. The fact was that Galland was now putting into action his own entirely unilateral and potentially very risky venture. Having discharged himself from hospital, he had set up his personal 'headquarters' in a villa on the shores of the Tegernsee, and had also secured a motorcycle and a Fieseler *Storch*. The latter machine was able to operate from a small piece of open ground not far from the villa.

In the early hours of the morning of 1 May, as he lay in bed, he typed out a note which he then sealed in an envelope and handed to Major Willi Herget, the former nightfighter ace, who, from this point on, would serve as his emissary. He instructed an astonished Herget to take the note in the *Storch* and fly to Schleissheim, in the northern outskirts of Munich, which was known to have been taken by the Americans.

At dawn, accompanied by Galland's aide, Hauptmann Kessler, Herget duly took off and flew low towards the city. Remarkably, he reached Schleissheim without attracting the attention of Allied fighters. The two Luftwaffe officers were met by curious and wary USAAF personnel. Stating that they were emissaries of Generalleutnant Adolf Galland, they asked to be taken to the most senior officer in the immediate area.

After about two hours, the Germans were driven to the Command Post of the 45th Infantry Division in the nearby town of Feldmoching. Here, they were presented to Gen Pearson Menoher, Chief-of-Staff of XV Corps, Gen Jesse Auton, commander of the 65th FW, Eighth Air Force, and Col Dorr E Newton, Deputy Commander of XII Tactical Air Command. Officers from the XV Corps Intelligence staff were also present, and personnel from the 45th Infantry Division acted as interpreters. Finally, a stenographer kept a record of who attended and what was discussed.

Herget handed over Galland's envelope and Menoher opened it. The letter it contained read as follows;

'From Adolf Galland (Generalleutnant)

'I have sent Major Herget as well as my personal aide, Captain Kessler, to the Commander-in-Chief of the Allied Forces in order to discuss with him the possibilities and terms of a special surrender of the last entire and fully operational jet fighter unit. I therefore kindly ask you to have me approached in this regard at the earliest possible time without any delay, since the destruction of the aircraft and special equipment as well as the disbandment of the unit should be expected at any hour.'

Herget and Kessler explained that Galland's proposal was based on the idea that if the jets were surrendered, their pilots could be used to fly sorties against the Russians. After a moment of bewilderment, the Americans composed themselves and checked with the Germans if Galland had sole authority to surrender *Jagdverband* 44, and whether they were clear about the fact that under the 'rules governing land warfare' as set down by the Geneva Convention, neither the men of a unit which surrenders nor its equipment could be used against its own people. The Germans replied that they were clear in this regard. Next, the Americans asked how long it would take for the Germans to return to Tegernsee.

'It would take about 45 minutes', Herget replied. 'We are not based at the field, as the General has been wounded and is in bed at a private place. We have no communications with the field, but we have a motorcycle.'

One of the representatives enquired, 'How long would it take General Galland to say "Yes" or "No" to unconditional surrender only? If you were to get back to him by 1530 hrs, could you be back here by 1730 hrs?'

'That is too quick', Herget replied. 'We could be back before dark tonight'.

There followed a detailed discussion as to exactly which American-occupied landing grounds JV 44's jets could be flown. The Americans even went as far as to discuss flight altitudes in clear and bad weather, and to offer an escort for the German aircraft along their route. But the Germans proved hesitant. Herget responded;

'If only unconditional surrender is acceptable, General Galland may order the aircraft destroyed on the ground. We also request that you do not use radio in discussing these details, as they will be intercepted and the aircraft will be destroyed by the SS.'

'That is Galland's decision to make', Menoher answered. 'Surrender is all I have the authority to offer. We will comply as far as possible in not using the radio. We are giving you these details for bringing in the aeroplanes in the event General Galland accepts'.

Menoher then offered to arrange to escort Herget and Kessler on their return flight with a pair of Piper L-4 'Cub' liaison aircraft, but he added, 'I would like General Galland to let us know today as to the acceptance or the rejection of this plan. Our escort will go as far as the frontline. If we can agree on a time, we will have two Cubs rendezvous at the place we leave them in order to pick them up when they come back.'

Herget nodded his understanding. 'We could do that. 1800 hrs would be a good time for the rendezvous.'

Menoher turned to an aide and drafted a note to Galland;

'To Lieutenant General Galland

'I have the authority to accept the surrender of *Jagdverband* 44 in accordance with the Rules of Land Warfare as prescribed by the Hague and Geneva Conventions. I am returning Major Herget and Captain Kessler to you with details of surrender attached. It is expected that they will return at 1800 hrs, this date, with your decision. I will arrange for their return air escort at that time.'

With that, Herget and Kessler returned to Schleissheim and departed in their *Storch* for Tegernsee, flanked by their escort of two USAAF Grasshoppers, through cloud-laden skies, heavy with the threat of snow. Well south of the city, the Grasshoppers turned for home, and some 30 minutes later, the *Storch* touched down at Tegernsee.

However, when Herget presented his bed-ridden commander with Menoher's response, Galland became disappointed. With the weather closing in over the mountains, he considered that to conform with the Americans' proposal to fly two formations of precious Me 262s using skilled pilots along the suggested routes of Salzburg to Giebelstadt (the former KG(J) 54 base south of Würzburg) and Innsbruck to Darmstadt (close to the Rhine) was unreasonable and impractical. Quickly, he drafted a polite, but brief reply to Menoher;

'To Brig Gen Pearson Menoher

'I thank you for the receipt of my couriers and for your declaration.

'The required execution of the action, however, fails because of the very bad weather conditions, the lack of fuel and, additionally, because of the technical problems with many of the Me 262 aircraft. I therefore rather suggest to again fix the terms for the special surrender of the whole unit (aircraft, spare parts, special ground support equipment, pilots and specialised personnel).

'I am at your disposal in that regard,

'Adolf Galland. Lt General.'

But it was too late. Snow was falling and it was too risky to allow Herget to fly the *Storch* in such adverse conditions. Galland waited until the next day, 2 May, by which time the weather had improved just enough to allow Herget to fly – alone – back to Schleissheim, carrying his reply.

As Herget once again approached the southern outskirts of Munich, the *Storch* was spotted by American ground troops who opened fire, suspecting that the low-flying German aircraft was about to launch an attack. Herget managed to crash-land the Fieseler and was promptly captured. He had suffered burns in the process and his captors quickly transported him to a rear area medical station for treatment. Herget's war was over.

At Tegernsee, Galland and Kessler waited – and waited. Eventually, having received no further news, the commander of JV 44 'decided to stay right where I was until I was overrun, and then start communications again'. Out of contact with Bär at Salzburg, there was nothing more to do but wait for the Americans to come. Galland's war was over too.

In the meantime, Me 262s had flown into Innsbruck-Hötting from Riem. By employing his workers day and night, Hans-Ekkehard Bob had done the best he could in the short time available to him, but the runway was still too short;

'As far as I can remember, about 12 aircraft arrived, one of which landed inadvertently on the old aerodrome with the short landing strip. The machine came to a standstill just in front of the aerodrome buildings. To this day, I do not understand why those aircraft were sent to Innsbruck, the more so because nobody could possibly think that they could have taken off again.'

Right and below
Two views of JV 44's Me 262 'White 1', which landed erroneously at Innsbruck's main civilian aerodrome at the end of April 1945. The style of markings suggest that the aircraft had originally been on the strength of *Kommando Nowotny*, **and may have been used as a training machine by III./EJG 2 prior to being passed onto JV 44**

With operational command of JV 44 now at Salzburg, Bob managed to establish a telephone link to Bär. Word came through that the Americans had reached Mittenwald, and were advancing through the mountains via Seefeld towards Innsbruck. Despite this news, Bob was given strict orders not to damage or destroy the jet fighters at Hötting, but rather to remove key components from their Jumo engines and prepare to conceal them somewhere the Americans would not be able to find them.

At some stage the telephone link was re-established between Galland and Bär, for Bär received an irate call from his commanding officer in response to an order from General Koller to move JV 44 to Prague. 'Don't move from where you are at Salzburg!' Galland yelled down the line. 'Stay there – don't move'. Bär understood. When one of Koller's staff officers from the OKL *Führungsstab* arrived at Salzburg to oversee proceedings, Bär's tactic was to ply the man with drink and persuade him to forget his orders. He was successful.

Further 'pressure' emerged in the forms of Generalmajor Dietrich Peltz, commander of IX. *Fliegerkorps*, and Oberst Hajo Herrmann, commander of 9. *Fliegerdivision*, who arrived somewhat unexpectedly at the control room at Maxglan in an attempt to bring Bär into line, and to order JV 44 to relocate. A heated argument ensued. Walter Krupinski, who was present, recalled 'there followed a violent dispute. At this time, we had learned through radio broadcasts from Prague that a Czechoslovakian uprising was already taking place. I recollect that during the argument in the flight control room, Generalmajor Peltz or Oberst Herrmann drew the Oberstleutnant's attention to the fact that they had given an order for the transfer to Prague-Rusin of one *Gruppe* of JG 300, which was based at Ainring airfield on the other side of the Saalach, and that this order was already being carried out.'

For a moment the discussions were drowned by the roar of engines overhead, as the last Bf 109s and Fw 190s of II., III. and IV./JG 300 took off from Ainring en route for Prague.

'As we were talking, Peltz said "Look, you see? They're taking off! They're going to Prague!", and Bär said something which I will never

Me 262 Wk-Nr. 111712 was another aircraft to reach Innsbruck from Riem. This particular machine was distinctive by virtue of its bare metal finish, with much of its surfaces covered by filler paste

Above and left
Representative of the overall green
overspray colour scheme of many of
JV 44's Me 262s was Wk-Nr. 500490,
seen here parked in the meadow
between Hötting airfield and the
road to Zirl

forget. "Yes, sir, but we are under the command of Generalleutnant Galland, and I will only follow the orders of Generalleutnant Galland!" I thought that they would shoot him there and then!'

Meanwhile, at Innsbruck, on the bitterly cold morning of 3 May, instructions were received to transport the removed Jumo engine parts by truck to Salzburg. Hans-Ekkehard Bob recalled;

'We reported by telephone that enemy tanks had already passed Seefeld, and that we were waiting to sight the first tanks, with our vehicles ready to move off. When we saw them approaching at a distance of some five kilometres from the airfield, I gave the order for the ground personnel to proceed quickly to Salzburg. The aircraft were left intact on the airfield, but without their regulators, which rendered them useless.

'On the evening of the same day, I arrived at Salzburg with my detachment and reported to Oberstleutnant Bär. Here too, I was told that the enemy was only a few kilometres from Salzburg. As I was equipped with lorries, I was firstly detailed to transport some consignments of food from the well supplied ration stocks at Salzburg. Our eyes nearly fell out at the sight of the delicacies in the ration stocks, the names of which we had almost forgotten! There were tins of meat, tins of fruit, chocolate, rice, filled biscuits and all sorts of sutlery items. As we knew from previous occasions, the officials were not willing to let us have anything. This "obstacle" was easily dealt with, and we were able to load our lorries with the most fantastic things.'

News of the extent of the American advance had reached Bär, but due to a further breakdown in communications, he was unable to contact Galland for further instructions. His last orders were to remain in force, as there were now virtually no alternative airfields to which JV 44 could move other than Prague and those in the east, which would mean almost certain Russian captivity.

The weather was deteriorating fast and fuel supply had now reached critical levels. In Bär's opinion there was only one viable course of action – to destroy the Me 262s on the ground. Reluctantly, he ordered Major Krupinski to make arrangements, but not before both officers had paid a visit to Unteroffizier Schallmoser in hospital to present him with the Iron Cross First Class. Schallmoser promised his superiors that he would be fit for action the next day.

Later that evening, Koller telephoned, concerned about the rumours he had heard. He recorded in his diary;

'Alarming news from Salzburg airfield that the enemy has reached the airfield and the troops want to blow up the Me 262s. It is night-time.

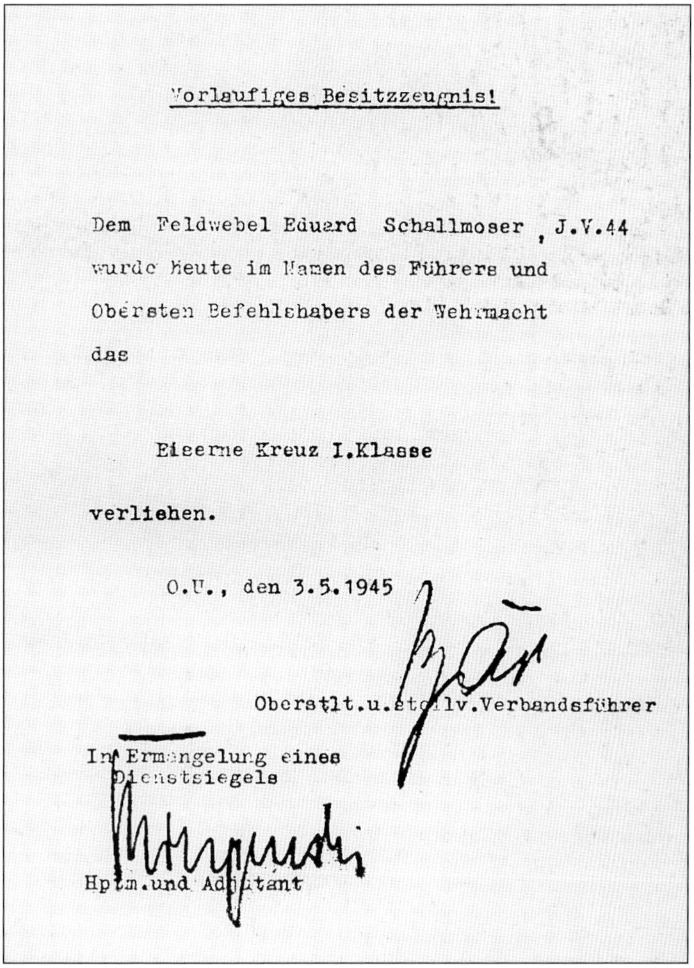

Vorläufiges Besitzzeugnis!

Dem Feldwebel Eduard Schallmoser , J.V.44 wurde heute im Namen des Führers und Obersten Befehlshabers der Wehrmacht das

Eiserne Kreuz I.Klasse

verliehen.

O.U., den 3.5.1945

Oberstlt.u.stellv.Verbandsführer

In Ermangelung eines Dienstsiegels

Hptm.und Adjutant

Unteroffizier Eduard Schallmoser's notice of the award of the Iron Cross First Class, dated 3 May 1945, and signed by Oberstleutnant Heinz Bär as acting *Verbandsführer* of JV 44 and Hauptmann Walter Krupinski as Adjutant

Seemingly incongruous amidst the spectacular mountain scenery towering above Hötting airfield is JV 44's Me 262 Wk-Nr. 111857. Bearing no tactical markings, the aircraft's distinguishing features are its prominent Werk Nummer and replacement cowlings around the engine intakes. Behind the Me 262 is Ju 87D-3 'E8+GL' of the night-harassment unit, NSG 9, complete with exhaust flame damper for nocturnal operations

Conversation with the *Kommandeur*, "There are no enemy troops on the airfield. The enemy can only be seen and heard west of the Saalach. The aircraft will not be demolished under any circumstances; we will try to transfer to Wels or Hörsching at dawn with the serviceable aircraft. Only such aircraft as are unserviceable and cannot be evacuated may be demolished".'

In a final attempt to bring JV 44 under control, Koller signalled another order to the effect that the *Jagdverband* was to reorganise itself immediately as IV./JG 7, and dissolve its existing command structure. Galland was to remain at the disposal of the Luftwaffe Personnel Office. It is unlikely, however, that much heed was given to any of these orders. JV 44 was no longer bothering to report strength and serviceability figures or mission reports. Communication with most of Germany was now impossible.

From Tegernsee, Galland sent a messenger to Salzburg with instructions for Bär to destroy all files and documents concerning the operations of JV 44.

As a cold dawn broke on the morning of 4 May, the pilots of JV 44 gathered for a final briefing in the snow-covered wooden barrack huts that served as their accommodation. From there they could watch American tanks massing on the far side of the Saalach. Bär gave Bob his final orders;

'The Americans were close to Salzburg airfield, which meant that we soldiers had to disappear. I was ordered to go with the lorries and a detachment of 16 men, well equipped with machine pistols and ammunition, and store the regulators safely somewhere in the mountains, and then to be available for the defence of the so-called '*Festung Alpen*' together with a detachment that was there already.

'I took the lorries and drove with my men roughly in the direction of Bad Ischl, and after four or five kilometres turned off into the mountains. I reached the village of Koppl, where the road ended. There were no soldiers in the village. I gave my men sufficient food and ammunition and dispersed them around the farms. Together with two pilots – two NCOs from JV 44 – I established my "Headquarters" at a farm located at the highest point in the village. Again we waited for something to happen, but nothing did.'

On the same day at Ainring, Heinz Sachsenberg instructed his Fw 190 pilots to destroy their personal papers, while the *Platzschutzschwarm's* equipment and other documents were loaded into a truck. However, before the vehicle was able to reach its unknown destination, it was destroyed by an enemy tank.

Back at Salzburg, the Americans had finished shelling the outskirts of the city. Then they broadcast announcements to all German units in the area to surrender, and to send representatives into the city. At this, Bär firstly instructed the groundcrews to remove the engine governors from the Me 262s, which would have the effect of immobilising the aircraft. Next, he ordered Major 'Bubi' Schnell and Fahnen-junker Oberfeldwebel Kaiser to form a delegation to investigate what was happening in the city. If possible, they were to return to Maxglan with an American representative with whom surrender terms could be negotiated. The remaining pilots then sat down to an early morning game of cards, and to await their fate.

A little later, at around 0715 hrs, Hauptmann Krupinski and a mechanic were doing their best to draw some warmth from the engine of a *Kettenkrad* tow-tractor to the eastern edge of the airfield. They had with them a box of hand grenades. Nearly two hours had passed by the time the American armour on the other side of the Saalach began to move, but having received no further word of an official surrender, Krupinski decided it was time to act. Firing up the *Kettenkrad*, the pair rode as fast as the little vehicle would take them along the line of Me 262s parked in the trees, placing grenades into the intakes of each engine. One by one, the grenades exploded, blasting the Jumo engines apart.

'The tanks suddenly stopped, and they must have wondered what was going on', recalled Krupinski. 'They must have thought that the war had started again! They didn't open fire. Maybe they had received a surrender notice by radio – but we hadn't'.

After 1100 combat missions, Hauptmann Walter Krupinski's last act of war was to sabotage the Me 262s of JV 44 at Salzburg-Maxglan as American forces approached the airfield

Armourers from the US Ninth Air Force enjoy an opportunity to inspect at first hand the 'business end'of an Me 262 of JV 44 at Innsbruck-Hötting shortly after the cessation of hostilities. Note the electric ignition cable attached to the lower 30 mm MK 108 cannon

From the huts, Unteroffizier Schallmoser watched his aircraft 'blow apart'. Fahnen-junker Oberfeldwebel Schuhmacher recalled that it was a sight that made the JV 44 pilots' 'hearts bleed'. One local resident heard the explosions and went to the window of his apartment from where he observed clouds of black smoke rising into the sky from the airfield.

Having completed their task, Krupinski and the mechanic rode back to the huts, leaving a line of smoking Me 262s behind them.

Eventually, the German pilots' card game was interrupted when the door to their hut was opened cautiously and an American GI, clutching a machine gun and chewing gum, peered into the gloom. One of the pilots shouted that he should have knocked first! The GI departed.

A little later Schnell and Kaiser arrived back at Maxglan in a jeep, accompanied by a US Intelligence officer. One by one, the senior officers – Bär, Krupinski, Barkhorn, Herget, Hohagen, Schnell, and Gutowski – were ordered to board trucks and were taken to Bad Aibling, where they would begin a long period of captivity and interrogation. Others, such as

Engine technicians of the US Ninth Air Force inspect the Jumo 004 jet engine of an Me 262A-1a of JV 44 at Innsbruck in May 1945

Mechanics of the US Ninth Air Force study the hydraulics on the nosewheel of an Me 262 of JV 44 at Innsbruck-Hötting. The stencilled marking on the nosewheel door reads 'ACHTUNG – Nicht am Bugrad Schleppen' (Attention! Do not tow by nosewheel). It was official practice to tow an Me 262 using a tow vehicle with cables fitted to lugs on the mainwheels

Klaus Neumann and Heinz Sachsenberg, together with Hofmann, Wübke and Dirschauer, made off, using whatever means they could.

Nearby, a determined Josef Dobnig had endured an almost epic journey from Munich-Riem to Salzburg in an attempt to rejoin his unit. Having survived repeated Allied bombing and strafing attacks, and passed through burning villages and endless retreating military columns, Dobnig decided to say farewell to his colleagues on the military lorry and cycle on alone to Salzburg. He did reach his destination, but it was too late. He was captured by American troops in the city.

Generalleutnant Adolf Galland surrendered himself to American forces at Tegernsee the next day, 5 May. Because of his knee wound, an American ambulance took him to the nearby town of Bad Tolz, where the US XXI Corps had set up its Command Post. On the 6th he met Col Dorr E Newton, to whom he had attempted to surrender JV 44 five days earlier. Galland told Newton, 'I have no place to go and no desire to go anywhere. I will be at your wishes at all times'.

USAAF Intelligence officers agreed to Galland's request to launch an immediate search for the remains of Günther Lützow, but the search around Donauwörth proved fruitless.

On 7 May 1945, 7. *Jagddivision* reported that 'JV 44 (Me 262 – IV./JG.7)' had been 'taken prisoner'.

Following an interrogation of Galland conducted on 14 May 1945, Maj Max van Rossum-Daum, the commander of the US 1st Tactical Air Force's Air Prisoner of War Interrogation Unit, based at Heidelberg, observed, 'In forming his unit, General Galland was determined to gather around him the very best that the GAF could offer. It was known in GAF circles that if you wanted to belong to *Jagdverband* 44, you had to have at least the *Ritterkreuz* (Knight's Cross).'

The myth of JV 44 had been born.

Pilots of the USAAF's 55th FG listen with interest as Generalleutnant Adolf Galland (centre), former *General der Jagdflieger* of the Luftwaffe and commander of *Jagdverband* 44, addresses them at Kaufbeuren airfield in August or September 1945 during his interrogation there. It is possible that this photograph was taken in an attic room of one of the airfield's accommodation blocks

APPENDICES

APPENDIX 1

JAGDVERBAND 44 PERSONNEL LIST, 27 APRIL 1945

Abschrift

```
Jagdverband 44                          Gefechtsstand,
BrTgb.-Nr. 80/45                        den 27.04.1985

KR-Fernschreiben


An

Luftflottenkommanod 6
- Lohengrin -


Betr.: Fernmündliche Rücksprache mit Major Schürmeier-
       Hptm. Gutowski vom 27.04.1945

I. Fliegendes Personal JV 44
     1. GenLt    Galland            Stab G.d.J.
     2. Oberst   Steinhoff          JG 7
     3. ObstLt   Bär                (Erg.)/JG 2
     4. Major    Barkhorn           JG 6
     5. Major    Hohagen            Nach Lazarett-Aufenthalt
     6. Major    Schnell            JG 102
     7. Major    Herget             Reisestab General Kleinrath
     8. Major    Brücker            I./KG 51
     9. Hptm     Kirchays           (Erg.)/JG 2
    10. Hptm     Esser              JG 102
    11. Hptm     Krupinski          III./JG 26
    12. Hptm     Wübke              II./JG 101
    13. OLt      Blomert            Fluglehrerschule der Lw.
    14. OLt      Stigler            (Erg.)/JG 1
    15. OLt      Faber              Stab G.d.J.
    16. OLt      Hondt              JG 11
    17. OLt      Walter             JG 105
    18. OLt      Richter            (Erg.)/JG 2
    19. OLt      Grünberg           JG 7
    20. Lt       Strate             I./KG 51
    21. Lt       Fuhrmann           (Erg.)/JG 2
    22. Lt       Bell               (Erg.)/JG 2
    23. Lt       Hofmann            (Erg.)/JG 2
    24. Lt       Fährmann           JG 7
    25. Lt       Neumann            JG 7
    26. Lt       Roth               III./JG 102
    27. Lt       Sachsenberg        II./JG 52
    28. Lt       Seufert            (Erg.)/JG 2
    29. Obfhr    Weindl             I./KG 51
    30. FhjOfw   Fröhlich           I./KG 51
```

-2-

This list was compiled by Hauptmann Werner Gutowski and reported to Major Schürmeir, an officer on the staff of *Luftflottenkommando* 6, on 27 April 1945. It is known to contain errors, as 'Hptm Kirchays' is believed to be actually Hauptmann Rüdiger von Kirchmayr, while 'Ofw Döring' is an erroneous reference to Oberfeldwebel Josef Dobni

-2-

31.	FhjOfw	Kaiser	Jagdfliegerheim Bad Wiesee
32.	FhjOfw	Schuhmacher	(Erg.)/JG 2
33.	Ofw	Klante	(Erg.)/JG 2
34.	Ofw	Döring	JG 103
35.	Ofw	Haase	JG 105
36.	Ofw	Knier	JG 101
37.	Ofw	Nielinger	JG 103
38.	Ofw	Reckers	JG 101
39.	Ofw	Schwaneberg	JG 103
40.	Fw	Kammerdiener	Flugzeugführerschule der Lw.
41.	Fw	Steiner	I./JG 11
42.	Fw	Trenke	I./KG 51
43.	Uffz	Pöhling	II./KG 51
44.	Uffz	Müller	Frontfliegersammelgruppe Quedl.
45.	Uffz	Schallmoser	(Erg.)/JG 2

Auf Anforderung des JV 44 sind keine Flugzeugführer bisher
kommandiert worden.

II. Vom JV 44 wurden keine Bild-Me 262 übernommen.

gez. Gutowski, Hptm.

APPENDIX 2

THE KNIGHT'S CROSS HOLDERS OF *JAGDVERBAND* 44

Name	Date of Award	Victories	To JV 44 from
Oberstleutnant Heinz Bär	Swo 16/2/42	approx. 220	III./EJG 2
Major Gerhard Barkhorn	Swo 2/3/44	301	JG 6 then hospitalised
Major Hans-Ekkehard Bob	KC 7/3/41	59	I. & II./EJG 2
Major Heinrich Brücker	KC 24/6/41	250 g/a missions	*Gen der Schl* & I./KG 51
Generalleutnant Adolf Galland	Dia 28/1/42	104	*Gen der Jagd*
Oberleutnant Hans Grünberg	KC 8/7/44	82	1./JG 7
Major Wilhelm Herget	Oak 11/4/44	63 (57 at night)	*Sond Komm Kleinrath*
Major Erich Hohagen	KC 5/10/41	55	III./JG 7 then hospitalised
Fhj Ofw Herbert Kaiser	KC 14/3/43	68	III./JG 1 then hospitalised
Hauptmann Rüdiger von Kirchmayr	KC 25/3/45	46	I./JG 11 (poss III./EJG 2)
Hauptmann Walter Krupinski	Oak 2/3/44	197	III./JG 26 then unassigned
Oberst Günther Lützow	Swo 11/10/41	108	*Jafü Oberitalien*
Leutnant Klaus Neumann	KC 9/12/44	37	*Stab* JG 7
Leutnant Heinz Sachsenberg	KC 9/6/44	104	II./JG 52
Major Karl-Heinz Schnell	KC 1/8/41	72	JG 102 then hospitalised
Fhj Ofw Leo Schuhmacher	KC 1/3/45	23	III./EJG 2
Oberst Johannes Steinhoff	Swo 28/7/44	176	*Stab* JG 7

Key

Dia – Diamonds to Knight's Cross

g/a – ground-attack

Gen der Jagd – *General der Jagdflieger* (General of Fighter Arm)

Gen der Schl – *General der Schlachtflieger* (General of Ground-Attack Arm)

Jafü – *Jagdfliegerführer* (Area Fighter Commander)

Fhj Ofw – Fahnen-junker Oberfeldwebel

KC – Knight's Cross

Oak – Oakleaves

Sond Komm – *Sonderkommission* (Special Commission)

Stab – Staff

Swo – Swords to Knight's Cross

1

Si 204D-1 'BM+JP' of JV 44, Brandenburg-Briest and Munich-Riem, March-May 1945

Used by JV 44 for twin-engined training purposes, and also as a transport, this aircraft was originally operated by the *Fluglehrerschule der Luftwaffe* at Brandenburg-Briest, and carried the unit's emblem (a red eagle with crown and swords) on the forward fuselage beneath the cockpit glazing. The fuselage code is in black, outlined in white, with a yellow fuselage band and the individual aircraft number '63' in white over both tail assemblies and rudders. The overall finish is a splinter pattern of 70/71 with undersides in 65. Several JV 44 pilots are believed to have flown in this machine, including Leutnant Blomert, Unteroffizier Müller, Oberfeldwebel Haase, Oberfeldwebel Nielinger, Oberfeldwebel Reckers and Feldwebel Kammerdiener.

2

Me 262A-1a Wk-Nr. 110556 'Red S' of JV 44, Brandenburg-Briest and Munich-Riem, March-April 1945

Built at Schwäbisch-Hall and believed to be one of the first aircraft on strength with JV 44, this aircraft was used for training, if not for operations, and is known to have been flown by Oberfeldwebel Josef Dobnig and Oberfeldwebel Rudolf Nielinger – the first Me 262 that each of these pilots flew. It has been finished in a splintered uppersurface camouflage of 81/82, which extends as a mottle over the fuselage, with a base of 76. The red 'S' is somewhat thin in style, and an unusual stencilled 'A4' appears twice on the forward fuselage/nose and in three places on the outboard side of the Jumo engine. The meaning of this stencilling is not known.

3

Me 262B-1a 'White S' of JV 44, Brandenburg-Briest and Munich-Riem, March-April 1945

The only known Me 262B-1a to be operated by JV 44, 'White S' was finished in a 81/82 scheme on the upper fuselage, with a fairly rigid demarcation line with the 76 base. A blotchy mottle of 82 was applied over the 76. Of note is the white *Hakenkreuz* on the tail.

4

Me 262A-1a Wk-Nr. 111745 'White 5' of JV 44, Munich-Riem, April 1945

Built at the Kuno AG *Werk* 1 at Scheppach (Burgau), this aircraft is known to have been flown by Unteroffizier Eduard Schallmoser and Unteroffizier Karl-Heinz Müller. 'White 5' was very representative of JV 44's core aircraft – the batch of Me 262s used by the unit when it first arrived at Munich-Riem. The jet was finished in overall 82, and featured only a white '5' – its tactical number – to distinguish it from other similarly camouflaged machines. Its *Werk Nummer* was stencilled in black beneath the *Hakenkreuz*.

5

Me 262A-1a/U4 Wk-Nr. 111899 of JV 44, Munich-Riem, April 1945

This Leipheim-built aircraft was painted in a standard late-war splinter pattern and mottle combination over the main airframe, although it appears a replacement rudder has been incorporated, possibly in 80 or 83. The specially fitted bare metal nose section housing the mechanism for the Mauser 50 mm MK 214 cannon was 'patched' with filler paste, and the actual panels holding the barrel appear to have been of a different metal to the rest of the nose.

6

Me 262A-2a Wk-Nr. 111685 'White F' of JV 44, Munich-Riem and the Hofoldinger Forest, April 1945

One of several aircraft from I./KG 51 which were posted to JV 44 in late April 1945, this Me 262 was built at Schwäbisch-Hall. It was finished in a somewhat unusual pattern of lightly applied areas of 81 over 82, particularly along the panel lines, while the undersides were in 76. The rudder – probably a replacement unit – appears to feature a base of a lighter green (possibly 82), with what appears to be 71 applied over it in a swirling pattern. The white tip of the tail assembly would have been applied later. The aircraft carries a fuselage code in a style relatively common to KG 51. It is likely that the bomb rack would have been removed when the jet was taken on by JV 44.

7

Me 262A-2a Wk-Nr. 110836 'Black L' of JV 44, Munich-Riem, April 1945

Built at Leipheim and taken on by JV 44 from KG 51 in late April 1945, 'Black L' featured tips to its nose and fin/rudder in black which may have denoted a former *Staffel* colour. The aircraft's individual letter 'L' is outlined in white, and appears to have been either a replacement letter code or the original letter repainted over a previous style. The 'L' was also applied to the nosewheel door. The usual bomb rack for an A-2a had been removed. This Me 262 was subsequently shipped to the USA, where it was coded as 'FE 110' and later given the name *Jabo Bait*.

8

Fw 190D-9 Wk-Nr. 600424 'Red 1' of JV 44 *Platzschutzschwarm*, Munich-Riem, April-May 1945

Featuring a blown canopy, this aircraft was built by Fieseler at Kassel and was finished in 82/83, possibly with an area of 81 over the cowling. The nose section of the spinner was painted yellow, with the rear section in black. The undersides were painted red all over, with white stripes unevenly spaced apart. Distinctive markings include a black and white quartered square enclosed by a red circle, which was common to all photographed machines of the *Platzschutzschwarm*, and the motto '*Verkaaft's mei Gwand 'I foahr in himmel!*' ('Sell my clothes, I'm going to heaven'). This aircraft is believed to have been flown by the leader of the *Platzschutzschwarm*, Leutnant Heinz Sachsenberg, while at Riem.

9

Fw 190D-11 Wk-Nr. 170933? 'Red '4' of JV 44 *Platzschutzschwarm*, Munich-Riem, April-May 1945

This Fw 190D-11 is believed to have been acquired by JV 44 from the *Verbandsführerschule General der Jagdflieger* (General of Fighters' Unit Leaders' School), based at Bad Wörishofen, not far from Munich. This unit was disbanded on 27 April 1945, and it seems that the aircraft made it to Riem just days before the elements of JV 44 transferred to Salzburg, Ainring and Innsbruck. It appears that the aircraft's uppersurfaces have been finished in an overall 75 grey – or even 77 – and then oversprayed in mottle of 82 and/or 83. Like the other aircraft in the *Platzschutzschwarm*, Red '4' had unevenly applied white stripes painted over red undersides, and carried a black and white quartered square enclosed by a red circle on the fuselage beneath the cockpit. Visible beneath the tactical red '4' is the white 'chevron 58' of its previous operator. The nose section of the spinner was painted yellow, with the rear section in black, and according to recent research, the *Werk Nummer* was in white. The pilot's personal motto was *Der nächste Herr dieselbe Dame!* (The next Man the same Woman!)

10

Me 262A-1a 'White 22' of JV 44, Munich-Riem and Salzburg-Maxglan, April 1945

Like 'White 5', 'White 22' was probably another of JV 44's early aircraft, and it was finished in overall 82, but with possible areas of 80. The tactical number '22' has been applied in a somewhat unusual squared-off style, and the aircraft has been fitted with a replacement rudder.

11

Fw 190D-9 'Red 3' of JV 44 *Platzschutzschwarm*, Ainring, May 1945

Carrying the motto *Im Auftrage der Reichsbahn* (By Order of the State Railway), this aircraft is believed to have been flown by Hauptmann Waldemar Wübke. It wears a scheme of 82/83 mottle (the 83 in large patches) possibly over a base coat of 77. The undersides were painted red overall, with white stripes varying in width and unevenly spaced apart. Beneath the cockpit is the *Platzschutzschwarm's* usual black and white quartered square enclosed by a red circle, while the nose section of the spinner was painted yellow, with the rear section in black. Note the slightly smaller than usual fuselage cross.

12

Fw 190D-9 Wk-Nr. 213240 'Red 13' of JV 44 *Platzschutzschwarm*, Ainring, May 1945

'Red 13' appears to have been finished in a blotchy 81/82/83 pattern on its fuselage uppersurfaces, with a mottle of 82 extending over the fuselage sides on a base of 77. This aircraft, which is believed to have been flown by Oberleutnant Klaus Faber, featured a spinner front nose section in yellow, with a rear section in black, and recent research suggests an earlier black and white spiral was just visible beneath the yellow. The *Werk Nummer* was in black and the aircraft carried the motto *"Rein muß er" und wenn wir beide weinen!* ('In he goes even though both of us will cry!'). Immediately beneath the cockpit is the *Platzschutzschwarm's* usual black and white quartered square enclosed by a red circle. Undersides were painted red overall, with white stripes varying in width and unevenly spaced apart.

13

Me 262A-2a Wk-Nr. 111712 of JV 44, Munich-Riem and Innsbruck-Hötting, April-May 1945

This aircraft was void of any colouring except for the uppersurfaces of its engine units, which were sprayed in 81, with feint mottling extending over the sides, which appear to have been finished in 76. A replacement rudder was also fitted, which again was finished in 81. The aircraft was given a black-bordered fuselage cross, and the last three digits of its *Werk Nummer* were applied to the very rear fuselage and in the area between the *Hakenkreuz* and above the horizontal stabiliser. While the tail unit was coated with primer, the rest of the aircraft had been left in bare metal, with the fuselage panel joints showing filler paste. As an Me 262A-2a, the aircraft would have been fitted with a bomb rack, and there was also head armour for the pilot.

14

Me 262A-1a 'White 1' of JV 44, Munich-Riem and Innsbruck-Hötting, April-May 1945

Quite how this aircraft ended up with JV 44 is not known, but from the camouflage pattern on the tail assembly (82 over 76), it would appear to have at one time been assigned to *Kommando Nowotny*, and perhaps even *Erprobungskommando 262*. The nose area features large areas of 81 sprayed over 82, while the pattern on the fuselage sides breaks down into more of a mottle of the same colours. The tactical number '1' forward of the cockpit was in white (this also appeared on the nosewheel door), while the band forward of the fuselage cross was in yellow. A small white 'S' was painted on the very rear fuselage beneath the horizontal stabiliser – evidence perhaps of a *'Schul'* (school) machine, which suggests that this may have been an aircraft joining JV 44 from III./EJG 2.

15

Me 262A-1a Wk-Nr. 500490 of JV 44, Munich-Riem and Innsbruck-Hötting, April-May 1945

Taken on by JV 44 from a batch of Me 262s undergoing completion work at the *Deutsche Lufthansa* facility at Munich-Riem and subsequently transferred to Innsbruck, this aircraft was finished in solid 83 over the fuselage uppersurfaces, ending in a marked, but wavy, demarcation line about a third of the way down the fuselage sides. At that point, the colour became mottled over a base colour of 75. The *Werk Nummer* was in black below a solid black *Hakenkreuz*, while the starboard Jumo engine unit had a replacement upper panel and intake casing left in bare metal.

16

Me 262A-1a 'White 4' of JV 44, Munich-Riem and Innsbruck-Hötting, April-May 1945

Typical of one of JV 44's core aircraft, 'White 4' was finished in overall 82, with its tactical number applied forward of the fuselage cross in the position favoured by the unit.

17

Me 262A-1a Wk-Nr. 111857 of JV 44, Munich-Riem and Innsbruck-Hötting, April-May 1945

In terms of colour scheme, this aircraft was representative of several of JV 44's core machines (see 'White 4', '5' and '22'), which suggests it may have been taken on by the unit during the first half of April 1945, but not assigned a tactical number. Of note is the prominent *Werk Nummer* in white and the bare metal replacement port side engine intake panel. This aircraft was built at Schwäbisch-Hall.

18
Me 262A-1a 'White 12' of JV 44, Munich-Riem and Innsbruck-Hötting, April-May 1945
This Me 262 displays the same somewhat unique squared-off style of tactical numbering as seen on 'White 22'. The jet, which ended up at Salzburg, appears relatively intact,

with no replacement panelling. It is finished in JV 44's typical overall 82, with the tactical number applied forward of the fuselage cross.

BIBLIOGRAPHY

ADERS, GEBHARD & HELD, WERNER, *Jagdgeschwader 51 'Mölders' – Eine Chronik*, Motorbuch Verlag, Stuttgart, 1985

BARBAS, BERND, *Die Geschichte der II. Gruppe des Jagdgeschwaders 52*, Bernd Barbas, undated

BOEHME, MANFRED *JG 7 – The World's First Jet Fighter Unit 1944/1945*, Schiffer, Atglen, PA, 1992

CALDWELL, DONALD, *The JG 26 War Diary Volume Two 1943-1945*, Grub Street, London, 1998

CALDWELL, DONALD & MULLER, RICHARD, *The Luftwaffe over Germany – Defense of the Reich*, Greenhill Books, London, 2007

O'CONNELL, DAN, *Messerschmitt Me 262 – The Production Log 1941-1945*, Classic Publications, 2005

CRANDALL, JERRY, *Doras of the Galland Circus*, Eagle Editions, Hamilton, 1999

DEBOECK, MARC, LARGER, ERIC & PORUBA TOMAS, *Focke-Wulf Fw 190D Camouflage & Markings Part 1*, JaPo, Hradec Králové, 2005

FORSYTH, ROBERT, *JV 44 – The Galland Circus*, Classic Publications, Burgess Hill, 1996

FORSYTH, ROBERT, *Jagdwaffe – Defending the Reich 1944-1945*, Classic Publications, Hersham, 2005

GALLAND, ADOLF, *The First and The Last*, Methuen, London, 1955

MANRHO, JOHN & PUTZ, RON, *Bodenplatte – The Luftwaffe's Last Hope: The Attack on Allied Airfields New Year's Day 1945*, Hikoki Publications, Crowborough, 2004

OBERMAIER, ERNST, *Die Ritterkreuzträger der Luftwaffe 1939-1945 – Band I Jagdflieger*, Verlag Dieter Hoffmann, Mainz, 1966 and 1982

PRIEN, JOCHEN & STEMMER, GERHARD, *Messerschmitt Bf 109 im Einsatz bei Stab und I./Jagdgeschwader 3*, Struve-Druck, Eutin, undated

PRIEN, JOCHEN, RODEIKE, PETER & STEMMER, GERHARD, *Messerschmitt Bf 109 im Einsatz bei Stab und I./Jagdgeschwader 27*, Struve-Druck, Eutin, undated

PRIEN, JOCHEN, *Geschichte des Jagdgeschwaders 77 Teil 3 1942-1943*, Struve-Druck, Eutin, undated

PRIEN, JOCHEN, *Geschichte des Jagdgeschwaders 77 Teil 4 1944-1945*, Struve-Druck, Eutin, undated

STEINHOFF, JOHANNES, *The Last Chance – The Pilot's Plot Against Göring*, Hutchinson, London, 1977

WEAL, JOHN, *Jagdgeschwader 52 – The Experten*, Osprey Publishing, Oxford, 2004

INDEX

References to illustrations are shown in **bold**.
Plates are shown with page and caption locators in brackets.

'*Aeropag*' conference 13-14
Allied Tactical Air Force, 2nd 18, 19
Anglo-Canadian 21st Army Group 111
Auton, Gen Jesse 112

Bad Wiesee, 'Florida' aircrew recuperation centre 19, 47, 50, **61**, 97
Bär, Obstlt Heinz 16-18, **17**, 19, 93-94, 107, 108, 115-116, **117**, 117, 118, 119, 120; at Munich-Riem 76, **77**, **78**, **79**, **93**
Barkhorn, Maj Gerhard 18, **61**, 61, 63, 71, 93, 120
bases: Autobahns **94**, 94, **95**; Bad Aibling 108, 109; Brandenburg-Briest 23, **33**, **36**, **37**; Innsbruck-Hötting 94, 96, **106**, 111, 114, **116**, **118-120**; Munich-Riem 37-38, **38**, **39**, 39-40, **52**, **54**, **58**, 58-59, **60**, **64-67**, 64, **78-81**, **93**, 100, **101**; Salzburg-Ainring **102-104**, 104-105, 106, 108, **109**, 115; Salzburg-Maxglan 94, 106-107, **107**
Baumbach, Obst Werner 78, 79
Below, Obst von 20, 22
Blomert, Oblt 28, 31, **33**, 36, 39, 63, **65**, **81**, **86**
Bob, Maj Hans-Ekkehard **110**, 110-111, 114-115, 116-117, 118-119
Bormann, Martin 78, 111
Brücker, Maj Heinrich **77**, 77, **79**
Bryner, 1Lt Charles E 88
Byrnes, SSgt Bernard J 89-90

Caldwell, Capt Lewis S **4**
Cowan, 1Lt Oliver T 84

Deutsche Lufthansa (DLH) 38, 110-111
Diesing, Obstlt Ulrich 12
Dietz, TSgt Henry 88-89, **89**, **90**
Dirschauer, Fw Bodo 100, 103, 121
Dobnig, Ofw Josef **29**, 29-30, **33**, 33-34, 36-37, 49, 121, 125; at Munich-Riem **54**, **65**, **79**, **86**, **96**, 96, 97
Dönitz, Adm Karl 75, 111

Estrada, SSgt Edmundo 72

Faber, Oblt Klaus **65**, **66**, **99**, 99-100, **100**, **103**, 108-109, 126
Fährmann, Lt Gottfried 28, 39, **40**, **47**, 52, 53, 67, 68, 107
Feldkirchen headquarters **48**, 49, 51, **63**, 63, 99
Finnegan, 1Lt James J **90**, 90, 91
Focke-Achgelis Fa 223: 108
Focke-Wulf Fw 190D **32**, 98, 101, 103-104
Focke-Wulf Fw 190D-9 **98**, **98**, 99, 101; 'Red 3' **11**(44, 126), **100**, **102**, **103**; Wk-Nr. 213240 'Red 13' **12**(44, 126), **104**, **105**, 108-109, **109**; Wk-Nr. 600424 'Red 1' **8**(43, 125), **101**, **102**
Focke-Wulf Fw 190D-11 **9**(43, 125-126), 101
Frisch, Fähnrich Gerhard 94
Frodl, Obst Ing. Franz 63, 92

Galland, GenLt Adolf 10, 10-11, **11**, 12, 14, **16**, 20-21, **24**, **25**, **81**, **83**; dismissal as *Gen der Jagdflieger* **16**, 16; forms Me 262 unit (JV 44) 22-26; and 'Free Bavaria' movement 96, 97; and Göring 8, 9, 10, 11, 12, **16**, 16, 22-23, 77-78, 79; and *Grosse Schlag* 9; and Me 262: 20-21, 22; and move to Munich-Riem 37, 38, 39; at Munich-Riem 48-49, 58-59, 60, 62-63, 64, 65, 66, 67, 76, 87, 88, 103; pilot training 31; and R4M rockets 57; recruiting pilots 32, 47-48, 49; and Salzburg-Maxglan 106, 108, 111, 115, 118, **119**; and tactics 35-36, 72; wounded 89, **90**, 90-92
Geyer, Hptm Horst **11**
Gollob, GenLt Gordon 14, 16, 20, 23, 25, **26**, 26, 49, 52, 99, 101
Göring, *Reichsmarschall* Hermann 8, **9**, 62, 75-76, 78, 108, 111; and Galland 8, 9, 10, 11, 12, 15, 16, 22, 23, 77-78, 79
Grabmann, Obst Walter 7, 12
Grünberg, Oblt Hans '*Specker*' **66**, 66-67
Gurkin, Capt Luther 88, **89**
Gutowski, Hptm Werner **49**, 49, 51, 63, 107, 120

Handrick, Obstlt Gotthardt 7, 10
Hansen, 1Lt James **73**, 73, **74**

Harms, 1Lt Fred J 81
Hartmann, Erich 37
Heinkel He 280 V7 108
Herget, Maj Wilhelm **61**, 61-62, **62**, 93, 97, 112, 113, 114, 120
Herrmann, Obstlt Hajo 8, 12, 115
Hitler, Adolf 8, 20, 22, 34, 61, 72, 78, 108, 111
Hofmann, Lt Karl-Heinz 39, **99**, **100**, 100, **103**, 108, 121
Hogan, TSgt Jack 89
Hohagen, Maj Erich 22, **27**, 27, 31-32, 39, **95**, 107, 120; at Munich-Riem 63, **65**, **66**, **67**, 71, **77**, **78**, **79**, **93**
Hondt, Oblt Erich **76**, 76-77, **77**

Jagdverband (JV) 44: established 24; first combat operation 36; *Platzschutzschwarm* (Airfield Defence Flight) **8**, **9**(43, 125-126), **11**, **12**(44, 126), **98-103**, 98-101, 103-105, 108-109, **109**; surrender 2-114, 120; tactics 71-72
Junkers Ju 87D-3 **118**
Junkers Ju 88: 108

Kaiser, Ofw Herbert **50**, 50-51, 63, **78**, **79**, 107, 119, 120
Kammerdiener, Fw Otto **28**, 28, 31, **33**, 35, 39, 57, 82, 91, 107, 125
Kammhuber, Genmaj Josef **34**, 34, 38, 61, 96, 97, 110
Kammler, *Dr. Ing.* Hans 75-76, 96, 97, 109
Kessler, Hptm Hugo 24, 63, 97, 112, 113, 114
Kirchmayr, Hptm Rüdiger von **49**, 49-50
Knier, Ofw Leopold 28-29, **33**, **40**, **78**, **79**, **81**, 107
Kogler, Obstlt Johann 7, 8
Koller, Gen Karl 12, 23, 24, 37, 75, 92, 109, 115, 117-118
Kornatzki, Maj Hans-Günter von **11**
Köster, Uffz Franz 87, 93
Krupinski, Hptm Walter **18**, 18-19, 47-48, 51-52, 53, 67, 68, 83, 85, 86, 93, 98-99, 100, **117**; at Munich-Riem **65**, **66**, **79**, **93**; at Salzburg 107, 115-116, 117, **119**, 119, 120
Luftwaffe: III./EJG 2: **17**, 18, 76; *Eprobungskommando* (E.Kdo) 25: **11**; *Jagdgeschwader* (JG) 4: 7-8; JG 7: 14, 24, 25, 39, 63, 92, 108; III./JG 7: 14, 22, 23; 10(N)./JG 26: 13; IV./JG 27: 7; II./JG 51: 30; II./JG 52: 108, **109**; IV./JG 54: **7**; JG 400: 25; II. *Jagdkorps*: I./KG 51: 77; 4./KG(J) 54: **70**, 70; 7./KG(J) 54: **70**; *Kommando Losigkeit* 33; *Kommando Nowotny* 14, **21**, 21-22; NSG 9: **118**; *Oberkommando der Luftwaffe* (OKL) 60, 93, 106, 115; *Schulungslehrgang Elbe* 8; *see also Jagdverband* 44
Lützow, Obst Günther 'Franzl' **15**, 15, **16**, 16, 19, 22, 77, 80, **82**, 83, 85, 85-86, 121; at Munich-Riem 62-63, **63**, **64**, **65**, **66**, **81**, 83

Maltzahn, Obst Günther von 15-16, **63**
Marseille, Fähnrich Hans-Joachim 13
Martin B-26 Marauder **4**, 72, **73**, 74-75, **75**, 80-82, **82**, 88
Mast, Capt Jerry G **84**, 84, 85
Menoher, Gen Pearson 112, 113
Messerschmitt, Prof Willy **9**
Messerschmitt Bf 109G **104**, **109**; Bf 109G-14 **8**
Messerschmitt Me 262 **4**, 20-21, 32-33, **37**, 51, **52**, **91**, **95**, 97, 98; III./EJG 2: **17**, 95; engines, Jumo 004 61, 69, 70; III./KG(J) 54: **70**; 70; *Kommando Nowotny* **21**, 21-22; 'White 6' **39**; Wk-Nr. 111074 **108**; *see also* weapons, Messerschmitt Me 262
Messerschmitt Me 262 V3 prototype **20**, 21
Messerschmitt Me 262A-1a **120**; 'White 1' **14**(45, 126), **114**; 'White 4' **16**(46, 126); 'White 12' **18**(46, 127), 88, **106**, 106; 'White 22' **10**(44, 126), **107**, 107; Wk-Nr 110556 'Red 5' **36**, **2**(41, 125); Wk-Nr. 111745 'White 5' **39**, **4**(42, 125), **52**, **55**, 57-58, **59**, 60; Wk-Nr. 111857 **17**(46, 126-127), **118**; Wk-Nr. 500490 **15**(45, 126), **116**
Messerschmitt Me 262A-1a/U4 **5**(42, 125), **62**, 87
Messerschmitt Me 262A-1/U-5 76, 93
Messerschmitt Me 262A-2a **6**, **7**(42, 43, 125), **13**(45, 26)
Messerschmitt Me 262B-1a **34**, **3**(41, 125)
Michel, Gefr Alfred **8**
Moench, Capt John O 87
Mölders, *Gen der Jagdflieger* Werner 11, 15
motorcycles, NSU *Kettenkrad* half-tracked 67, **68**, 92, 119
Müller, Uffz Johann-Karl 'Jonny' **28**, 28, 39, 57-58

59, 60, 74, **75**, 107, 125
Myers, 2Lt William H **84**, **85**, 85

Neumann, Lt Klaus 34, **35**, 36, 39, **65**, **66**, **67**, 67, 76, 83, 107, 120-121
Newton, Col Dorr E 112, 121
Nielinger, Ofw Rudolf **30**, 30, 35, 39, 53, **65**, 66, 106, 125
North American B-25 Mitchell **7**
Nowotny, Maj Walter 14, **21**, 21, 22

Operation *Bodenplatte* 6-8, **7**, **8**, 9, 12, 19

Peltz, Genmaj Dietrich 7, 8, **12**, 12, 22, 115

Quong, Sgt Jonny 83

Radlein, TSgt Robert M 72-73
Republic P-47D Thunderbolt **85**, **90**
Rödel, Obst Gustav 15
Roell, Maj Werner 61, 110
Rossum-Daum, Maj Max von 121

Sachsenberg, Lt Heinz **98**, 98-99, **99**, **100**, 100, 101, **103**, 103, 108, 119, 121
Sagebiel, *Prof. Dr.-Ing.* Ernst 37, 40
Sanders, 1Lt Dale E 72
Schallmoser, Uffz Eduard **30**, 30-31, **33**, 35, 52-53, **59**, 66, 88, 91, 107, **117**, 117, 120, 125; at Munich-Riem **39**, 39, **54**, **60**, **65**, **66**, **68**, **79**; shot down **73**, 73-74, **74**, 75
Schnell, Maj Karl-Heinz '*Bubi*' 26, **27**, 63, 107, 119, 120
Schrader, Oblt Karl-Heinz 50
Schuhmacher, Fhj Ofw Leo 76, **77**, **78**, **79**, **81**, **86**, 88, 107, 120
Schwaneberg, Ofw Siegfried 29-30, 33-34, **77**, **78**, **79**
Shatto, 1Lt Alf P 88
Siebel Si 204: **31**, 31, **101**; Si 204D-1 **1**(41, 125)
Smith Jnr, 2Lt Byron 84-85
Sorrelle, 1Lt John W 88
Späte, Maj Wolfgang 25
Speer, Albert 20, 78-79
Stalter, 2Lt James L 83-84
Stamp, Maj Gerhard 22
Steiner, Ofw Franz **32**, 32-33, **33**, 35, 39, **79**, **81**, 107
Steinhoff, Obst Johannes 'Macki' **13**, 13, 14-15, 17, 19, 22, 24, **25**, 26, 27, 35, 36, 39, **47**, 47, 53, 54, 67, 86, 93, 97; at Munich-Riem 51, 63, **64**, 64, **65**, **66**, 68-70, **69**, **70**; and R4M rockets 57
Stigler, Oblt Franz **35**, 35, 39, 67, 71, **77**, **79**, 107

Tank, Dr Kurt **15**
Trautloft, Obst Hannes 16, 26, **63**
Trubenbach, Obst Hans 7
Truver, SSgt Edward F 81, 82

US Army: Seventh Army 106; 45th Infantry Division 112; *see also* Anglo-Canadian 21st Army Group 111
US Army Air Force *see also* Allied Tactical Air Force, 2nd 18, 19
    air forces: Eighth 47, 53, 57, **58**, 67, 71; Ninth **4**, 67, 71, **119**, 120; Twelfth 47; Fifteenth 47, 52, 67, 71
    bomb groups (BGs): 17th 80-81, **82**, 87-90, **89**; 232rd 82-83; 323rd 72-73, **73**, 74-75, **75**, 87; 344th 82-84, 87; 379th 53, 54
    bomb squadrons (BSs): 34th 81-82, **82**; 432nd 88, 89-90; 454th 72-73, 73, 74-75
    fighter groups (FGs): 27th 90; 50th 90; 55th **121**; 353rd 60; 365th 83, 84-85
    fighter squadrons (FSs): 10th **90**; 90; 388th **85**

Vining, 1Lt James L 74-75

weapons, Messerschmitt Me 262: cannon, MK 108 30 mm 22, 52, **53**, **119**; cannon, MK 214 50 mm **5**(42, 125); 62, 87; rocket, R4M 55 mm 54, **56**, 57
Weissenberger, Maj Theo 14, 24, 25, 34, **35**
Wills, TSgt Cleo E 88
Wübke, Hptm Waldemar **99**, **100**, 100-101, **103**, 108, 121

Young, Sgt Warren E 80-81